The Customer-Focused Library

The Customer-Focused Library

Re-Inventing the Library
From the Outside-In

Joseph R. Matthews

Libraries Unlimited

An Imprint of ABC-CLIO, LLC

A B C ⬛ C L I O

Santa Barbara, California • Denver, Colorado • Oxford, England

Library of Congress Cataloging-in-Publication Data
Matthews, Joseph R.
  The customer-focused library : re-inventing the library from the
    outside-in / Joseph R. Matthews.
        p. cm.
  Includes bibliographical references and index.
  ISBN 978-1-59158-875-7 (pbk : alk. paper) ISBN 978-1-59158-876-4 (ebook) 1. Public
libraries—United States. 2. Public services (Libraries) 3. Library
users. 4. Libraries and community. 5. Libraries—Marketing. 6.
Organizational change. I. Title.
Z731.M339 2009
027.473—dc22   2009026359

13 12 11 10 9   1 2 3 4 5

This book is also available on the World Wide Web as an eBook.
Visit www.abc-clio.com for details.

ABC-CLIO, LLC
130 Cremona Drive, P.O. Box 1911
Santa Barbara, California 93116-1911

This book is printed on acid-free paper ∞
Manufactured in the United States of America

10 9 8 7 6 5 4 3 2 1

Contents

Acknowledgments

As anyone who has written a book will attest, the final product is the result of the contributions of many talented people. It has been my good fortune to have been hired as a consultant by a number of librarians, which has led to the opportunity to visit a great many public libraries. I have also had the opportunity of working with a wonderful librarian and building consultant, Ray Holt, on a number of projects. Ray always believed that the public library could transform lives and that it was important to design and build libraries that inspired those who lived in the community.

In am also indebted to a number of friends and colleagues who took the time to read drafts of this book and make many useful comments and suggestions, which clearly benefit the contents. The comments of Diane Satchwell, assistant library director of the Oakland (CA) Public Library, and Diane Bednarski, principal librarian at the Santa Monica (CA) Public Library, were particularly helpful.

In addition, those who gave generously of their time include Anthony Bernier, assistant professor at the School of Library & Information Science at San Jose State University; Larry Nash White, assistant professor at the Department of Library Science and Instructional Technology at East Carolina University; Richard Dougherty, professor emeritus of the School of Information at the University of Michigan. Ivan Chew of the Singapore Public Library.

My thanks also to Sharon DeJohn for once again making my initial efforts more readable. Her careful and thoughtful editing is the mark of a true professional. And I would be remiss if I did not mention the ongoing encouragement that I receive from Sue Easun and Ron Mass of Libraries Unlimited. It is appreciated.

Any errors, faults, and limitations of this work are obviously mine and should not reflect upon those listed above.

Joe Matthews
Carlsbad, CA

Introduction

As you read this book, it is my hope that you will experience a number of reactions and emotions. I hope that you will be

- joyful—when you discover something new;

- in pain—when you recognize your library has a long way to go;

- hopeful—when you realize your library can be great;

- delighted—when your library staff start the journey forward;

- troubled—when you realize that the journey is going to take time and require a good deal of work;

- thrilled—when you learn of the experiences of your peers around the world;

- optimistic—that you and your library staff have the talent and energy to meet the challenge;

- aching—when you talk to your customers and feel their pain and frustration when they attempt to use your library;

- elated—when you see some staff who "get it" and begin to look at the library from the outside-in;

- angry—(hopefully not with me, although you might be), but that's OK, because you are thinking about the future of your library and what it might be, which is my intent;

- jubilant—when staff come to you with some suggestions of how to involve customers in developing a new service;

- anxious—when you consider the amount of change the concept of a customer-focused library is going to require;

- encouraged—by the successes of other customer-focused libraries;

- concerned—that the process of becoming a customer-focused library is not a project but an ongoing journey; and

- challenged—when you realize that your library can become a great library but the process will require leadership.

CHANGE IS IN THE AIR

Organizations, including libraries, are subjected to a tremendous amount of stress that causes them to change. Among the many forces that cause this change are economic conditions, the rapid pace of change in information technology, and competitive

> *The beginning of knowledge is the discovery of something that we do not understand.*
> —Frank Herbert[1]

pressures. The result is that many for-profit firms, governmental agencies, and nonprofit organizations have gone through a process of redefining and reinventing themselves over the last 20 plus years.

The future is less and less about the extrapolation of the past, because change is accelerating. As libraries confront the forces that compel change, they can choose between two possible paths: the *reactive path*, on which librarians take a back seat and vigorously resist change and thus have fewer choices about the consequences of change and therefore about what the library becomes over time, and the *proactive path*, on which librarians and customers *together* help coinvent the future that will provide a library that really adds value in the lives of their customers.

The public library in many communities is increasingly being marginalized. Yet in others the public library continues to play a vital role and, in fact, is becoming increasingly more relevant. A library is much more than a building. What has changed is that the library is no longer a warehouse for materials. People can get books and other materials, information, and other services that libraries provide from many other sources. The key to the future is for libraries to respond by offering a distinctive service and experience that builds on their historic strengths.

As a profession, we must identify unexamined dogmas, unexploited trends, unseen assets, and unvoiced needs. In short, we need to reinvent the public library.

A library has a choice about the way it arranges and provides access to knowledge and other cultural resources. It is possible to develop new configurations of books, information, electronic access to resources, and related services that can be delivered in a variety of ways and through a range of media.

Among the many drivers of change especially worth noting are shifting socioeconomic characteristics, advancing technologies, economic concerns, social interaction, environmental concerns, economic trends, and do-it-yourself attitudes.

SHIFTS IN SOCIOECONOMIC CHARACTERISTICS

The demographic characteristics of a great many communities are in the process of changing, often quite dramatically. This change has been called "demographic churn." As new immigrants find their place in American society, and as citizens move for professional, family, or personal reasons, U.S. communities are also changing. As Bob Dylan noted in his classic song many years ago, "The times they are a-changin'," and this observation is still relevant today.

Public libraries continue to provide access to the Internet and other information technologies to the economically challenged. The economic divide continues, and some suggest it is expanding. The library provides a safe place for people to learn about technology and how it can be used to improve their lives. However, simply acknowledging that change is occurring, without a fundamental reconsideration of the role of the library in the lives of those whom the library serves, is not acceptable.

ADVANCING TECHNOLOGIES

Change in the technology arena is likely to be faster, and perhaps less predictable, than ever. Broadband, Wi-Fi, and mobile technology all contribute to the increasing speed and availability of direct Internet communication, and so far libraries have been reasonably able to keep pace (although this is more problematic for smaller libraries). The challenge for any library is not to be on the "bleeding edge" of technology while at the same time not being such a laggard that the library is viewed as a museum of "dead and dated" technology. This is a difficult balance to maintain.

Google and other search engines are spending sizeable amounts of money to digitize a significant number of the books found in very large academic libraries. These projects scan each page and convert the scanned images into text that then becomes searchable (see, e.g., Google Books). And as the volume of electronic text continues to increase relentlessly day by day, the need to physically visit libraries will decline—often significantly. In addition to the growing number of digitized books, publishers are also releasing e-books, which must also be included in an assessment of providing access to digital resources. Thus, the traditional value model for any library of providing access to books, artifacts, and other resources, is in the midst of radical change.[2] And it is important to remember that convenience trumps almost everything!

The ready availability of information on the Internet and its immediacy of access have had a tremendous impact on all types of libraries. The Online Computer Library Center (OCLC) report *Perceptions of Libraries and Information Resources* found that a majority of people look first to search engines, and that the library is often the "court of last resort," if it is even on the radar screen at all![3] People are relying on other approaches to information, and the need for intermediaries is diminishing.

A very large set of computer-related resources is becoming increasingly available via the Internet in which the data and the software applications are both to found on the Net. This network-centric phenomenon is sometimes called "the cloud" or "cloud computing." Be aware that cloud-based services, such as Google docs and similar applications, will only increase their share of the market. Perhaps your library will need fewer copies of MS Office residing on desktop computers, and the majority of library computers will use OpenOffice (no cost) applications. If your data are stored in the "cloud," they become accessible from work, home, and while traveling, using a variety of devices.

People are more connected than ever and are using devices that are converging, as exemplified by the iPhone. Whether via a cell phone, a PDA, a Blackberry, or a laptop, people are using wireless as a way of staying connected with their work, friends, and family.

The Internet fuels a great deal of speculation about the concept of something called Web 2.0. Although there is a fair amount of hyperbole about this artificial assignment of numbers, Web 2.0 is all about connecting people in new ways, such as participation in content creation, co-creation or collaboration, tagging, syndication, mashups, and rich interfaces that enable a library to venture beyond the HTML page. In a broader library context, Web 2.0 has been called Library 2.0, which suggests that the discussion is all about attitude and much less about specific technologies. It's about relaxing control over the data, the interface, and the experience while continuously improving with the help of customers. It's about developing platforms that enable participatory, user-driven services.

The increasing use of and reliance on technology to deliver services—in the library and virtually—means that the library is becoming more dependent on reliable technology. It is likely that the library will need to spend more on technology to ensure that it is operational 24/7.

SOCIAL INTERACTION

Libraries are facing real competition, especially from larger bookstores, which market themselves as places to spend time with a good book and a cup of coffee, offering children's story times, hosting book author talks, helping to download digital content, and so forth. Clearly having a relaxed experience in a comfortable setting has great appeal. But for a great many libraries, especially public libraries, the competition is "eating our lunch." Library offerings are perceived as less varied, flexible, and more rule-bound than those of bookstores and cafes. And the same is true in the online environment. Users of Amazon.com have the opportunity to rate and review books and see suggestions about what to read next

The "library as place" offers the opportunity for individuals and various groups from a community to interact for a variety of reasons. Whether through the traditional children's story hour, small group study spaces, book discussion groups, an interaction with a reference librarian, attending a technology class, or even the nontraditional use of gaming, such as Wii, among teens (or even the boomers who are becoming seniors—some of whom prefer to be called "zoomers"), the library provides the opportunity for conversations and social interactions to occur.

A great deal of social interaction, often called *social networking*, is taking place using the Internet. The popularity and use of such sites as MySpace, Facebook, Friendster, Second Life, and many, many more are simply amazing and continue to grow at staggering rates. The Internet facilitates sharing: pictures (Flickr), knowledge (Wikipedia), videos (YouTube and Bebo), selective filtering (Digg), organizing content (del.icio.us), views on many subjects (blogs), ratings (Technorati), distribution using Real Simple Syndication or RSS, and much, much more. And although librarians may be concerned about the reliability of the data being shared, the reality is that people—more and more people—are using these and similar sites every day!

ENVIRONMENTAL CONCERNS

Libraries, by their very nature, are a classic illustration of recycling—the collective provision and reuse of books, recorded music, videos, and DVDs rather than individual ownership. In more recent years libraries have provided access to Internet computers, which helps bridge the gap between the technological haves and have-nots in contemporary society.

When a library is designing a new building or remodeling an existing facility, it can be much more environmentally friendly in the choice of building materials and landscaping, as well as in its fundamental design. The Leadership in Energy and Environmental Design (LEED) Green Building Rating System™ encourages the adoption of sustainable green building and development practices. A building can be LEED certified at various levels—gold, silver, and so forth. A library can be an environmentally friendly role model for its community when it builds new or remodels existing buildings.[4]

ECONOMIC TRENDS

The economies of countries around the world have gone through up and down cycles, and the United States is certainly no exception. Almost everyone would agree that we are in the midst of an economic crisis. With the problems in the housing industry and higher crude oil prices, and the prices we pay at the gas pump, every nation's economy is going to encounter problems. We have also seen dramatic price increases for food and a variety of commodities.

Historically, public libraries have seen an increase in use of their collections and services as people seek to improve their job skills and find resources of value. And as the economy tightens in various communities, it will not be surprising for a library to face the demand to reduce its budget. The need to reduce a library's budget can be an opportunity to reexamine its existing services and identify those that are infrequently used and thus can be eliminated.

There clearly are segments of a community's population that are less than supportive when it comes to financially supporting a library. The recent OCLC report *From Awareness to Funding* revealed that use of the library is only marginally related to financial support for the library.[5] Another key finding is the belief that a library should be a transformational force in people's lives.

DO-IT-YOURSELF ATTITUDES

Individuals are becoming increasingly self-sufficient. People are using the Internet to shop for the lowest price for a product or service. Self-service, in which we scan our own purchases at checkout lines, is being used by numerous stores. Thus, we are interacting with institutions differently. Rather than using traditional "middlemen," consumers are going direct to the source much more frequently. This phenomenon, called "disintermediation," is having a dampening effect on traditional library services.

There is tremendous interest in developing skills such as learning how to cook, build and remodel homes, repair cars, and so forth, as evidenced by the popularity of stores such as Lowes and Home Depot and programs on the Food Network and Home & Garden Television. And although libraries have provided collection resources to meet the information needs of the do-it-yourself (DIY) crowd, they have done little to organize speakers or demonstrations about how to accomplish a specific task or activity.

We also see this DIY approach in many of the most-viewed sites on the Internet, leading to the "cult of the amateur," in which popular content is produced by nonprofessionals. Just consider some of the more popular user-created content Internet sites, such as Wikipedia, YouTube, and Flickr.

WHAT TO DO?

The challenge for any library is to acknowledge all of these forces that are having an impact on society and the individuals in our communities. It is also important to acknowledge and understand that each of these forces is having and will continue to have significant consequences for your library.

Thus, it is imperative that we begin to design new libraries, whether building new buildings or remodeling existing facilities, with the customer in mind. But as we will see in the next few chapters, this is not an easy task. We may think that if a library is "good," it should only be a matter of making a few minor changes to get to "better." Unfortunately, this is not the case.

Consider the differences between the traditional library focus and a customer focus:

Library Focus	Customer Focus
Library shelving designed for maximum storage	Bookstore shelving and fixtures designed for maximum accessibility
Just-in-case collections	Just-in-time collections
The warehouse	The marketplace
Print collections	Multimedia collections
My library's collection	Library without walls
Build a "what they will need" collection	Give 'em what they want
Precoordinated subject headings	User tagging
Users need instruction	Make systems smarter and easier
Library-focused newsletters	Customer-created blogs
Go to the library	Services anywhere, anytime
Control the catalog	Encourage users to write reviews
Rules that restrict	Enable users to accomplish what they wish
Integrated library system	Web 2.0 + services
Library-controlled content	User-created content
Focus of mission is output	Focus of mission is outcomes
Predictability	Embracing change
Focus on the past	Focus on the future—of the community
Altruism	Return on investment
Perfectionism	Good enough is good enough
The exception	A part of the mainstream
Come to the library	Google it!
Rigidity	Flexibility
Complacency	Urgency
Information	TRANSFORMATION

Remember—

The world is going to change with or without you . . .

and

If you don't like change . . .

GET READY!

You're going to like *irrelevance* even less.

This book is all about getting a library to

Reinvent

Rethink

Redefine

Refocus

Redesign

Rediscover

REBRAND

Refresh

Reimagine

(Be) Remarkable

RESTRUCTURE

Reassess

RECONCEPTUALIZE

Realign

Reawaken

Reengineer

REENGAGE

REGENERATE

REEXAMINE

(Be) Relevant

Readjust

REBUILD

Reappraise

Rebound

Recharge

Reclaim

Recognize

Recommit

Re-create

Redeploy

REENERGIZE

REFINE

Rekindle

REMAKE

Renew

Retool

Renew

Retrofit

Reevaluate

Revive

and not

Recede

Reduce

Regress

Retrench

Repeat

ORGANIZATION OF THE BOOK

The intent of *The Customer-Focused Library* is to explore ways in which libraries have historically organized their collections and services and then to suggest that it is time to consider a radical alternative—designing library buildings, collections, and services from the customer's perspective, or from the

outside-in!

This book is organized to help you think about where libraries have been and how we currently think about library buildings, the provision of services, library Web sites, and online resources.

Chapter 1—Traditional Library Thinking

Over the course of time, librarians have developed a long list of traditions, which shape what services are offered, how services are delivered, how libraries are organized, how services and activities in the library are referred to and described (sometimes called *library speak*), and so forth.

Chapter 2—The Constraints of Tradition

Traditions can be both liberating and a cause for celebration, but can also constrain how we think about libraries and the services we provide. The extent to which these blinders of tradition (sometimes called "sacred cows") limit the possible ways libraries could or should serve their communities is explored in this chapter.

Chapter 3—It's All About the Customer

This chapter reviews a number of different ways in which a library can categorize or segment its potential user population. In addition to the traditional approach of using demographic information, developing customer groups based on benefit segmentation is recommended as a way to reveal a much more helpful picture of the library's customers and their needs.

Chapter 4—Library as Place

After a historical review of the evolution of branch facilities and their relationship to the central or main library, the importance of the library as a destination is discussed at some length. Alternative types of libraries that have been created are identified and reviewed.

Chapter 5—The Library Collection

This chapter explores alternative ways in which a library can store and make accessible it physical collections. Important issues such as the classification system, type of shelving, and organization of the library are addressed.

Chapter 6—Library Services

What services a library should offer in response to the needs of a community is an important concern. However, how these services will be provided is a much more important topic, which is rarely addressed when a library is engaged in the planning process. Alternative service delivery options are explored in this chapter.

Chapter 7—Information Technology

Information technology is playing an increasingly important role in our lives, and this is especially true for any public library. Yet most library online catalogs and Web sites are simply horrible. What can be done to improve them? And how will the increasing amount of digital content be made available to members of the community using the library's online catalog and/or Web site? This chapter discusses these issues.

Chapter 8—Library Staffing

This chapter is about the need to recruit, develop, and excite staff for the amount of change that will be required in the library and in their lives if the library is to become customer focused. Related issues of providing high levels of customer service, and staff uniforms, are also considered.

Chapter 9—Removing the Shackles of Tradition

A challenge to walk the walk from the customer perspective starts off this chapter. The importance of focusing on the customer and developing an outside-in discipline so that the needs of the customer inform every decision the library makes is considered. Acknowledging that there will be some resistance to change will help the library embrace innovation. A discussion of the importance of design is also provided.

NOTES

1. Quoted in Keith R. McFarland, *The Breakthrough Company: How Everyday Companies Become Extraordinary Performers* (New York: Crown Books, 2008).

2. Mark J. Ludwig and Margaret R. Wells, "Is the BISON Catalog Going the Way of Its Namesake?" *Library Journal* 133, no. 11 (June 15, 2008): 30–32.

3. Cathy De Rosa, Joanne Cantrell, Diane Cellentani, Janet Hawk, Lillie Jenkins, and Alane Wilson, *Perceptions of Libraries and Information Resources* (Dublin, OH: OCLC, 2005).

4. William M. Brown, "Building for Relevance and Flexibility Can Ensure Your Library Will Be There to Help Patrons Navigate Rapidly Changing Times," *Library Journal* 133, no. 15 (September 15, 2008): 1, 8–10.

5. Cathy De Rosa and Jenny Johnson, *From Awareness to Funding: A Study of Library Support in America* (Dublin, OH: OCLC, 2008), 1–6.

Traditional Library Thinking

Stability and continuity are no longer characteristics that can be used to describe the library profession. The profession is now best characterized by change, discontinuity, and opportunity.
—Robert Stueart and Barbara Moran[1]

People who cannot invent and reinvent themselves must be content with borrowed postures, secondhand ideas, fitting in instead of standing out.
—Warren C. Bennis[2]

For a long time, libraries felt that they enjoyed something of a monopoly in providing access to information. Despite the "advance" of moving from closed stacks to open stacks, the perception of a library among the public was that it was a place staffed by librarians who shushed when things got too noisy. But the monopoly, if there ever was one, has clearly been broken, and the search engines on the Internet are clearly the preferred place where people go for information. Today, the vast majority of information searches begin not at a library reference desk or online at a library Web site, but rather at an Internet search engine—especially Google.[3]

A large-scale survey conducted on behalf of the Online Computer Library Center (OCLC) asked respondents to compare search engines and libraries in four areas: quality of information provided, quantity of information, speed of conducting research, and overall experience. The search engines beat libraries in every category—sometimes by wide margins.[4]

In any profession, and certainly this is true for librarians, a fair amount of momentum is built up over time about how things "should" be done. Why is it that no matter what type of library it is, the same kind of library shelving is utilized? Why is it that no matter the type of material, many libraries simply use the shelving that was designed for the spine-out display and storage of books for CDs, DVDs, kits, and so forth? Why is it that libraries are reluctant to use a "new" (to the library) vendor?

Why is it necessary to catalog an item using *Anglo-American Cataloging Rules* (AACRII) or the more recently adopted *Functional Requirements for Bibliographic Records* (FRBR), which result in long, intricate records? Why has the library profession not looked at the evidence that only a small portion of the long cataloging records (records that used to be called full MARC records) are actually used? Why do libraries still insist that items added to a library's catalog must utilize a long bibliographic record—despite the high costs associated with cataloging an item and the evidence that only a small part of the record is used for retrieval? The adherents to traditional long bibliographic records and the value of the complicated library catalog have become believers in biblio-fundamentalism. Finally, why do catalogers believe so strongly in "bibliographic control?"

Why do libraries insist on maintaining "special" collections that are rarely used or still rely on card- or print-based tools to gain access? Why are libraries reluctant to stop providing access to services that are hard to use and seldom used by the customer—for example, microfilm readers/printers?

Why do professional reference librarians spend their time at a service desk? These reference librarians spend a great deal of their time sitting and waiting for someone to approach their service desks. They may spend their time waiting reading professional literature, reading reviews, being immersed in e-mail, surfing the Net, and so forth. Yet when someone does approach, chances are quite high that his or her question will be a directional one or one that does not require extensive training to provide the answer. In short, this seems like a tremendous waste of time for a highly paid professional. Does sitting at a reference desk really involve adding value for the library's customers? Do hospitals put doctors in the waiting room to wait for sick patients?

Why are reference desks constructed in such a way that they are imposing and unwelcoming? Why is the print reference collection so large when there is clear evidence that few of the volumes are ever used? Why is the reference service called "reference?"

Looking at a library and what it does is clearly going to be affected by perspective. For example, imagine that you are on vacation and have rented a cottage on the seashore. If you are inside the cottage (say the living room, with a view of the lawn leading down to the sand, the waves, and the ocean), the extent and direction of the view will be controlled by the size and placement of the windows and any walls, trees, or shrubs that may interfere with the view. More than likely the view will be quite nice, and you will be pleased with what you see. You are experiencing the seashore from an inside-out perspective. If, however, you were on the outside walking around the cottage, you not only would see the same nice view, but you would also see what is on either side and in the back of the cottage. From the outside-in perspective the cottage might be idyllic or a remnant of a bygone era—perhaps now the cottage is situated close to industry and a busy highway. Thus, one's perspective can have a powerful influence on how one views an organization—such as a library.

Almost all libraries rely on traditional spine-out shelving, for a simple reason—efficiency. This type of shelving means that the greatest number of books and other items can be stored in the smallest area. This high density of materials also means that libraries must be built with reinforced concrete floors that are considerably thicker and stronger and more expensive than those found in a typical office building. From the customer's perspective, materials located on the highest and lowest shelves are difficult to browse or to find specific items. (Let's find a footstool so I can find the desired item on the top shelf!)

The vast majority of libraries are organized with an inward-looking perspective. The collection is organized using the Dewey Decimal classification system in a public library and the Library of Congress classification system in an academic library. Other classifications systems may well be used in other types of libraries. However, although these systems do organize the library's collection, they can be a bit daunting to understand, with lengthy numbers occurring after the decimal point, or require sorting through a combination of letters and numbers to find the shelf location.

In some cases, a library's nonfiction collection is broken up into two or more subject areas, with their corresponding service desks, which makes wayfinding (the ways in which people orient themselves in physical space and navigate from place to place) a much more difficult task.

Once the customer has acquired the call number for a desired item(s), he or she then faces the challenge of navigating or wayfinding around the library to find the required item(s). The library may provide some signage, which may be helpful or not, but often the wayfinding clues are difficult to discern and interpret. Thus it may be necessary to find a staff member, which can be difficult because a lot of libraries do not ask their staff to wear identification badges or a uniform shirt.

The signage in the library may be confusing. Consider signs that identify collection subject areas but provide no clue to how the collection is organized using a range of call numbers—and the customer has a call number in hand. The library's response to the confusion experienced by customers as they attempt to find materials on the shelves (or in the stacks) is to put up posters and create brochures, handouts, and other documents that attempt to decipher the classification system of choice in the library.

So the experience of visiting the library, from the customers' perspective, may be frustrating because they may be required to overcome a series of obstacles to find the desired item(s). These obstacles include the following:

- **The library's catalog**, which treats every search request quite literally rather than using the approach a search engine employs, which is to find and present useful items on the first screen or two based on a relevance algorithm.

- **The library's subject headings**, which are created in a foreign language—the *Library of Congress Subject Headings*. For example, a search for "space shuttle" will fail because the "authorized" subject heading is "reusable space vehicle."

- **Signage**, which in libraries with multiple floors may make getting to the general area where the desired item is located difficult. The signage and general lack of a map at key wayfinding points may prove really frustrating.

- **Stack signage**, which may sometimes be confusing and reflect a library focus (e.g., using library jargon such as FIC to indicate fiction) rather than using everyday words.

- **Finding the item's actual shelf location using** a specific call number in a mix of short and long call numbers, which is especially difficult with a long string of numbers after the decimal point.

- **Discovering the desired item is not on the shelf**, which happens for a variety of reasons. It may have been borrowed by another customer, have been misshelved, be waiting to be reshelved, be lost or "missing in action," and so forth. This is particularly bothersome when the status of items is not updated in the library's catalog. In general, customers only find what they are looking for about 60 percent of the time.[5]

Confronted by these and other obstacles, it is not surprising that the typical customer will more often than not leave the library without asking for help and not have the desired item in hand. Of course, this assumes that the library customer has not made an error in copying the call number correctly—which is not always the case.

The library must figure out how to become woven into the fabric of the lives of their customers. The customer fabric includes more than just lending books, or CDs, or DVDs, or . . . . The library must learn to communicate in a more meaningful way with its customers so that there is a discussion about the lives of the customers and their needs and about how the library could better meet those needs. Such a conversation implies collaboration rather than the library relying on the "field of dreams" approach to providing service: "If you build it, they will come!"

John Moore asks an interesting question in his blog *Brand Autopsy*: "Would you miss _____ (fill in the blank with the name of a company, organization, or your library)?"[6] So, would you miss Crate & Barrel? Or would you miss UPS? Well, you get the idea. So, with apologies to John:

> Does *your public library* provide such a unique service and customer experience that we would be saddened if it didn't exist?

> Does *your public library* treat its employees so astonishingly well that those workers would not be able to find another employer to treat them as well?

> Does *your public library* forge such unfailing emotional connections with its customers that they would fail to find another source of the desired services that could forge just as strong an emotional bond?

> Does *your public library* rely on the "power user" who has mastered the intricacies of the library rather than simplifying and improving the experience of using the library for the majority of people?

> Has *your public library* created such deep connections with different customer segments that your customers would be dismayed if the library were to close permanently?

Such questions do give one pause for thought (and, yes it's true—the thoughts can be a bit depressing)!

Yet many librarians will cite new services they are providing, such as Internet accessible computer workstations, instruction programs to learn computer programs such as word processing, spreadsheets, and so forth, as evidence that libraries are being innovative and are adapting to the changing times. These and any other add-on services will not, by themselves, provide an enduring justification for public libraries. Public service renewal requires strong political leadership to confront complacency, set ambitious goals, and nurture innovation.

One real challenge for public librarians is that America has too many small libraries! These libraries may have been in the right places at one point in time, but they are not in the right places for twenty-first-century society. Transforming these small, in-

If you won't face today's reality, you will be trapped in yesterday's delusion.
—Michael Kanazawa and Robert Miles[7]

flexible, poorly designed, independent libraries into places that are vibrant and fills a need in each of our communities is a challenge that must be addressed head on. And of course these small libraries often have vocal advocates for preserving the past. At times it is difficult for the public as well as librarians to "let go."

Over the course of time, librarians have developed a set of services and created collections based on a set of assumptions about whom they serve and the needs of the community. These assumptions or perspectives might be considered a paradigm, as suggested by Thomas Kuhn.[8] A paradigm is a worldview that encompasses a set of broadly and deeply held beliefs, in this case about what a public library is and ought to be. Librarians become prisoners to a library-centric paradigm, and this limiting view is also held by some customers, who are wed to the traditional definition of the library as a quiet place to read and reflect.

In this book, I am calling for librarians to break the chains of this library-centric paradigm and develop a new worldview that has the customer at its heart. It is time for a library paradigm shift, for some out-of-the-box thinking to create libraries that are much more responsive to the differing needs of various market segments. It is time for us to reinvent the library from the

The definition of insanity is continuing to do the same thing and expecting a different outcome.

—Albert Einstein

outside-in!

NOTES

1. *Library and Information Center Management* (Westport, CT: Libraires Unlimited, 2007), 464.

2. Warren Bennis and Robert Townsend, *Reinventing Leadership: Strategies to Empower the Organization* (New York: Collins Business Essentials, 2005), 47.

3. Cathy De Rosa, Joanne Cantrell, Diane Cellentani, Janet Hawk, Lillie Jenkins, and Alane Wilson, *Perceptions of Libraries and Information Resources* (Dublin, OH: OCLC, 2006). See also Cathy De Rosa, Joanne Cantrell, Janet Hawk, and Alane Wilson, *College Students' Perceptions of Libraries and Information Resources* (Dublin, OH: OCLC, 2006).

4. Cathy De Rosa, Joanne Cantrell, Diane Cellentani, Janet Hawk, Lillie Jenkins, and Alane Wilson, *Perceptions of Libraries and Information Resources* (Dublin, OH: OCLC, 2005).

5. See chapter 8 of Joseph R. Matthews, *The Evaluation & Measurement of Library Services* (Westport, CT: Libraries Unlimited, 2007).

6. Visit John Moore's blog at http://brandautopsy.typepad.com/brandautopsy/would_you_care/index.html.

7. *Big Ideas to Big Results: Remake and Recharge Your Company, FAST* (Upper Saddle River, NJ: PT Press, 2008), 33.

8. Thomas S. Kuhn, *The Structure of Scientific Revolutions* (Chicago: University of Chicago Press, 1966).

The Constraints of Tradition

Traditionalists are pessimists about the future and optimists about the past.

—Lewis Mumford[1]

Over the course of time many organizations, including libraries, slip into a comfortable, routine view of themselves, their services, and their customers. This inward-looking perspective is strengthened by the fact that many librarians only read a little of the professional literature and have only a slight incentive to embrace a broader view of their libraries and the services they provide. Even fewer in the library profession routinely read journals presenting articles about technology, marketing, business, organizational development, advertising, design, customer service, and so forth. Therefore it is not surprising to find that librarians are inwardly focused. In addition, the tendency of the library profession to attract those who are introverts and have a desire for control further strengthens the inward-looking, library-centric perspective.

Although libraries have responded to the changing external environment, especially influenced by information technology, as evidenced by public computers that provide access to the Internet, libraries by and large are very similar to what they were 10, 20, 30, or more years ago. Materials are purchased for the collection, cataloged, and stored on traditional library shelving in spine-out call number order. In a public library the collection is usually divided into children's, young adult, and adult fiction and nonfiction. Audiovisual media are typically separated by type of media.

Why do libraries spend so little time and effort communicating to their communities the realities that their buildings are often cramped and out of date and that it is thus difficult to provide space for new materials, new media, new services, and technology? Why do librarians simply shrug their shoulders when confronted with the reality that they will be providing services from a really crummy building for another 10, 15, or 20 years?

Why do librarians have difficulty with the fact that "less" can mean more? There is a reluctance to weed seldom-used items to provide space for face-out shelving, walkable isles, lower shelving to improve line-of-sight views within the library, and so forth. This may in fact

7

be a reflection of the "just in case" mentality of librarians: We need to keep the collection large just in case someone might need something . . . sometime in the future.

Why do librarians fail to realize that libraries are complex and that, other than the "power user," most people visiting the library have a challenging task finding the resources they are interested in quickly and easily? Several studies have shown that a majority of library visitors actually spend between 10 and 15 minutes visiting the library (having only a general idea of what they want). Yet the library is organized as if most library customers will use the online catalog, identify items of interest, note the call number, visit the stacks in hopes the desired item is on the shelf (which it is only about 60 percent of the time), and then check out the items. Please! The majority of people simply want to browse the collection to find something of interest.

Libraries typically use signage that is difficult to understand due to the use of library jargon and complicated numerical systems (Dewey Decimals) to organize resources. The net result is that those in the know, aka librarians and other staff members, have no difficulty navigating the information space called the library, but those who have yet to crack the code, aka average people, become frustrated— and may not return.

Sacred cows make the best hamburger.
—Mark Twain

Branch libraries may "own" their collections, and some materials may not be shared with other locations—even if they are not used—unless specifically requested by a customer!

Reference librarians are available at a service desk to assist patrons in answering questions or finding materials in the library's collection. Yet these highly trained and highly paid professionals spend a great deal of their time at the desk waiting to provide a service. And when a customer approaches, it is often to ask for directions!

Programs are developed and held for preschool children and adults, yet most libraries are reluctant to prepare a cost-benefit analysis of the effectiveness of offering these programs. Compared to the total number of members of the community or registered borrowers, the number of program participants would not even reach 1 percent—and likely less than .1 percent. Yet the prospect of figuring out how to make such programs more relevant in the lives of community members and reach a greater audience is never considered. Is it possible to provide such programs online as a video or audio file that can be downloaded?

A summer reading program is provided and promoted, and libraries find that they are fairly busy during the summer. Although a large number of children may start the program, the drop-off rate can be quite high, and less than 50 percent may finish. The literature reveals that no library evaluation study has attempted to contact those who dropped out to find out why. Perhaps the reading theme does not resonate with and engage the children? Perhaps the incentives do not motivate the children? Are the parents of the children aware of the benefits that follow from participating in a summer reading program? Can children participate in an online manner?

Marketing of the library is viewed as less important because marketing is defined as providing bookmarks at the circulation desk. The marketing budget in most libraries is nothing— zero.

Why do libraries spend 10 percent or more of their budget purchasing new materials, only to have the items sit in technical services for weeks or months before they are placed on the shelves so customers may borrow them? Why do libraries place so many stickers on an item? Why is so much information about an item coded and abbreviated? For example, what are "FIC," "YA," and numerous other abbreviations that libraries use all about? And what does "Easy Reader" mean?

Materials

Materials are loaned for a period of time that varies by type of media and age of the borrower. Fines are typically charged to encourage the return of materials (the "big stick" theory), but the library will still lose a fair amount of loaned material (and revenue) because these items are never returned. Libraries do send overdue notices, but the wording of such notices fails to become stronger over time—despite the fact that the people with materials that have been overdue for more than six to eight weeks are likely to never return these items.

Some libraries charge a fee to place a hold or to borrow a specific type of material, such as DVDs. Providing a list (of holds) to be able to read a best seller is not a service—especially if the customer has to wait months to lay hands on the book. And libraries call this "good customer service"? The customer wants the book—now!

Why do library systems with branches spend a fortune moving materials around from branch to branch? Why must an item returned at one location be transported to its "owning" location? While all these items are in transit, they are unavailable for a library customer to borrow. The costs and the impact on the environment made by moving these materials are significant: Why can't a floating collection work? Well, it's tradition!

Most libraries charge a small fee to limit the demand for interlibrary loan. The fact that it may take several weeks for an item requested using interlibrary loan is not only acceptable but one of the intended by-products of limiting demand for the service.

One of the requirements for a librarian is to periodically weed the collection. However, weeding is one of those things that simply is given a very low priority and thus is hardly ever done on a regular basis. Despite the ready availability of data from the library's circulation system to identify items that have not been borrowed in years, librarians feel that shelves that are "bursting at the seams" are a good thing.

Why do libraries spend so much of their budget on electronic resources, only to identify them by the name of the provider? From the customer's perspective, what the heck does ABI/INFORM, ProQuest, Ebrary, Emerald, Ingenta, JSTOR, EBSCOHost, or OmniFile do for me? What will I find if I choose one of these products? Why not describe what I get so that when I select one of these products, I'm likely to find something of value? After all, it is the end user—the customer—who is being asked to make a choice when he or she is online. Perhaps this is one of the reasons people choose to Google it!

Why do libraries promote the fact that they provide Internet access and then prohibit young customers, or customers of any age, from using a social network site such as MySpace or Facebook? Why do libraries have signs that say "Turn your cell phones off" or "Using a cell phone in the library is prohibited"?

Why do libraries promote online access to reference librarians and then say that the librarian will attempt to get back to the customer within 48 hours? Why are limits placed on the number of online reference requests per week? If the same customer walked in the door, the assistance would be provided immediately!

Library security systems are used to reduce theft of materials, but the reliability of the systems is questionable due to a high number of false alarms. However, it is believed that it is important to perpetuate the myth that the security system works, even though regular library users are aware that these systems simply do not work well, if at all.

Why do libraries make it so difficult to pay fines and fees? Cash is king! Want a drink on Southwest Airlines—you need a credit card. Even the Salvation Army is taking credit cards! And if your library takes credit cards, people can make a donation to the library on your Web site using a credit card. Why not?

Why do libraries have so many detailed rules, procedures, regulations, policies, and standards? Most of the rules are designed to allow a library to say "no." How often have you heard a library staff member say, "Well, the library policy is . . . ." More often than not these policies get in the way of providing excellent customer service! Why do staff members fall back on reciting policy rather than using their good judgment to arrive at a win-win situation? A new staff member can be trained to work with policies in a matter of weeks, whereas learning the nuances of the job and developing a suitable basis for making sound judgments can take years. Libraries need to explore options such as mentoring and immediate performance feedback to help build a staff capable of exercising sound judgment while working within the organizational framework.

Too often libraries assume that the value of a library in a community is understood by the members of the community and especially by the funding decision makers. Libraries have spent very little time trying to document the value of the library in terms that will resonate with city council members, city managers, and county administrators. As a result, when a budget crunch occurs, the library is often the first, and in many cases the only, department asked to makes cuts to its budget.

> If *Library Journal* wrote an article about the success of your library in
> three to five years, what would it say?

Have you ever noticed that a great many police departments are rewarded for failure? How can that be? Well, crime goes up, and the police department is rewarded with a budget increase!

Why is it that the library profession has so many fanatics in its midst? Consider these familiar figures:

The *bibliographic control fanatic*—We need full bibliographic records.

The *"pure" cataloging fanatic*—We can't allow reviews, ratings, or tagging by customers.

The *perfection fanatic*—"Good enough" is never good enough.

The *balanced collection fanatic*—Never-read classics must sit on the shelf "just in case."

The *open standards fanatic*—XML is truly awesome.

The *open source fanatic*—Linux is the answer.

The *vendor fanatic*—Our next release fixes all your problems.

The *Web 2.0 fanatic*—Can you do 23 things?

The *instruction fanatic*—Library instruction is the key.

The *information fanatic*—Forget Google; we have quality.

The *searcher fanatic*—Boolean searching is always the answer.

The *signage fanatic*—We need a sign to explain everything, especially the rules.

The bottom line for most library staff members is that the library exists because it is a good thing. Everyone knows that—right?

NOTES

1. *Faith for Living* (New York: Harcourt, Brace, 1940), 51.

It's All About the Customer

The heart of what strategy is about is creating value for customers.
—Kenichi Ohmae[1]

Not surprisingly, the primary focus of an outside-in organization is the customer. An outside-in library starts with, and always returns to, the customer. The library should develop, in its "mind," a very clear picture of the customer and recognize that it in fact needs to develop many pictures—one for each customer segment. Often, librarians bring many assumptions to the planning process about the needs of different customer segments, without subjecting those assumptions to examination. These assumptions skew the planning process, and the result is a library facility and a set of services that simply do not resonate with the customers.

WHAT'S IN A NAME?

Historically, a majority of public libraries have called their customers either *users* or *patrons*. For example, many libraries refer to their library cards as "patron cards." In my mind, the choice of the name used by a library to refer to its customers is very important. Consider some of the names that libraries use to refer to their users:

- *Patrons* are individuals who champion someone or something and can be thought of as sponsors or benefactors. Yet very few library patrons ever donate money to a library. Librarians will suggest that their use of *patron* is appropriate because these individuals are supporting the library through their use of the library's collections and services. But such library usage in no way reflects the meaning of the word *patron*.

- *Users* are considered by many to be those who have embraced the drug culture. In a library setting, users are those individuals who are already making use of the library. These are individuals who have learned the "lay of the land" and know where to find resources and services they are interested in.

- The term *borrowers* emphasizes the fact that the library loans materials to those individuals who physically visit the library. The term is much more difficult to apply to those who avail themselves of electronic services and resources provided by the library virtually.

- The terms *card holders* or *registered borrowers* highlight the fact that some proportion of the potential service population has visited the library and obtained a library card. But there is no link between being a card holder and use of the library.

- The term *readers* emphasizes the fact that most people who use the library do so to obtain reading materials. Some people enjoy the fact that the library provides space and furniture so that they can read in the library. The term is used infrequently in U.S. libraries and is more likely to be used in England.

- The term *clients* stresses the relationship between an individual and a professional advisor who delivers a high level of personal or professional services, for example, management consulting or financial audit services. The term is more likely to be used in a special library setting and is rarely used in an academic or public library setting.

- *Member* is a term that some libraries and library users use to describe themselves. Many people use it to describe their relationship to gyms, video stores, online communities, store loyalty clubs, and so forth.

- *Guests* is a term frequently used in the hospitality industry—hotels, restaurants, and amusement parks (Disney and others). Some libraries that are focusing on high-quality customer services are embracing the term for users of the library.

- The term *customers* emphasizes the fact that the individuals using the library actually "pay" a real cost (distance to travel to the library, time to visit the library physically or virtually, etc.) and thus must actually make a "purchase" decision. The use of the word *customer* reminds library staff members that individuals are choosing to visit the library and that they have customer service expectations that must be met or exceeded. In fact, in many cities and counties, it could be argued that library customers are the "ultimate" customers because they have already paid for the service through their taxes.

How library staff members refer to their customers is, in my view, an important issue that deserves much discussion in every library. What *do* you call your library visitors? What *should* you call your library visitors?

WHO IS YOUR CUSTOMER?

The first step in focusing on your customers is to ask the most obvious question, "Who is the customer?" Who uses the library's physical or electronic resources and services? Who among the library nonusers might become a customer? How can the nonuser be reached most effectively?

Knowing who your customers are is very important for a library. Ask a library director or librarian who the customers are, and almost without exception you will receive a response indicating that the "average" customer is male or female, from a particular ethnic group, of a known age, and so forth. Ask the librarian why the customer uses the library, and he or she will likely respond with "to attend a program," "to borrow books or DVDs," and so forth. But the question then arises, "How closely do the perceptions of the librarian actually match reality?"

What data are available to answer that question? The librarian could examine the registered borrower file in the library's automated system. For a public library, the number of registered borrowers will include citizens from within the city or county being served as well as some number of borrowers who live outside the jurisdiction's boundaries. However, there are some problems with this "total registered borrowers" number. Most libraries purge their borrower files annually, deleting those registered borrowers who have not used the library in the last three years. Few libraries distinguish between the number of those who live within the jurisdiction and the total number of borrowers. Thus, if a library calculates a percent of registered borrowers compared to the number of citizens within the city or county, the result looks much better than it really is.

The registered borrower file has been used to create two broad types of analysis to gain a better understanding of the library's customers. First, some libraries have used the borrower file in conjunction with a geographic information system (GIS) to discover where each customer lives and by implication learn about the customer's socioeconomic characteristics using the available census data or "lifestyle" demographic data from commercial firms.[2]

A number of studies have demonstrated that population characteristics such as education, family lifestyle, and physical proximity to a library have more to do with use than do age, sex, and ethnic background.[3]

A second approach is to analyze the population by *use*, which results in the often referred to split between users and nonusers. Using the report capabilities of the library's automated system, it is possible to sort the registered borrowers into several groups:

- *Customers* are registered individuals with a library card. These individuals can be subdivided into three broad groups:

  - *Frequent customers* are those who use the library on a monthly or more frequent basis. Research suggests that in general about 80 percent of a library's circulation can be accounted for by 20 percent of the library's customers (the actual percentages may be slightly off in some libraries). The 80/20 rule in a library setting was first noticed by Richard Trueswell, and has also been called the Pareto effect. Joseph Juran called this effect the "vital few and the trivial many."

  - *Moderate customers* are those who use the library bimonthly.

  - *Infrequent customers* are those who have used the library sometime during the past year.

- *Lost customers* are individuals who visited the library, completed an application form, and received a library card. However, they have not used the library in the past year. Thus, although they "found" the library at one time, they are now "lost."

  One of the real limitations of a library's integrated library system is that it does not help the library keep track of other uses of the library—attending programs, reading newspapers and magazines, using Wi-Fi, and so forth. This is a challenge that vendors must start addressing soon. And libraries must get creative in tracking such usage in meaningful ways.

  Almost all organizations that spend any money on marketing know that it is easier to attract "lost" customers than it is to attract a noncustomer—often by a factor of 50. The costs to attract a "lost customer" to return to the library are considerably less than trying to attract nonusers who have never visited the library before. Given that the library has contact information for their lost customers (name, address, telephone number, and, in most cases, an e-mail address), it is quite simply amazing that libraries do not use this information to communicate on a regular basis about what is "new" about the library. Attractive and regular e-mail could be sent to these lost customers to encourage them to find their way back to the library.

It is true that many individuals refuse to provide their e-mail addresses due to privacy concerns. The library must persuade the customer of the benefits of potential future contacts and then live up to those expectations. The customer should be able to establish different levels of contact—overdue notices only, new materials alerts, forthcoming programs, and so forth.

A recent analysis of library customer satisfaction survey data revealed that it takes as many as 20 visits to the library before an individual develops the library "habit" and becomes a very satisfied (and frequent) customer.[4]

- *Nonusers* are people within a community who may or may not be aware of the location of the library and the range of services that it offers. Joan Frye Williams has called nonusers "civilians."[5] Note that these civilians can be divided into two groups: those who can be enticed to the library and those who will never, under any circumstances, use the library.

One study in a public library setting found that lost users and nonusers alike did not use the library due to distance, inconvenience of hours, and their preference to purchase their own materials. Further analysis revealed that adding to the collection in each location would entice lost customers to return, whereas building more locations and adding more hours would attract nonusers to the library.[6]

Another way to visualize use of the library is to conceptualize the level of customer involvement in library services, as shown in Figure 3.1. Low-involvement services depend on the facilities available and on individuals who typically serve themselves. A customer who only uses the library's electronic resources would be another example of a low-involvement customer. Medium-involvement customers are those who use the collections intensively but typically have little or no interaction with library staff members. High-involvement customers are those who have a high degree of interaction with librarians, collections, and the facilities.

A survey of 661 public library customers in Taiwan found that about 77 percent of the customers were low-involvement, 20 percent were medium-involvement, and only 3 percent were high-involvement. An analysis of customer satisfaction found that high-involvement customers focused on staff empathy, medium-involvement customers were interested in the availability of materials, and low-involvement customers were interested in the amenities of the physical space.[7]

BENEFIT SEGMENTATION

For libraries that are interested in adopting an outside-in perspective to better understand customers and their needs, it might be more fruitful to understand what benefits they receive from a physical or virtual visit to the library. That is, the package of likely benefits that results from a use of the library will be different for each market segment of the population. The primary advantage of segmentation includes

- a better understanding of customers and their needs and

- a more effective targeting of resources.

High Involvement	Use of electronic resources
	Use of librarian-mediated reference
	Interlibrary loans

Medium Involvement	Use of reference collection
	Borrowing of books and other media
	Photocopying

Low Involvement	Program attendance
	Browsing magazines and newspapers
	Using facilities for personal study

Figure 3.1. User Involvement with Library Services. Adapted from Pao-Long Chang and Pao-Nuan Hsieh, "Customer Involvement with Services in Public Libraries," *Asian Libraries* 6, nos. 3/4 (1997): 242–49.

The market segments would be defined by the primary use of the library rather than relying on demographic information. A pilot study at the Dover (Delaware) Public Library resulted in identifying eight identity-related reasons for a visit to the library:[8]

- *Experience seekers* look to the library as a venue for entertainment or social connection. They like being around people and may be seeking an activity to occupy their time. (Selected by 36 percent of the respondents.)

- *Explorers* are individuals who are curious and love to learn but do not have a specific topic or subject agenda prior to the visit. (Selected by 35 percent of the respondents.)

- *Problem solvers* have a specific question or problem they want to solve. They might be looking for health information or investment information, be planning a trip, and so forth. (Selected by 23 percent of the respondents.)

- *Facilitators* are individuals who are there to support someone else in their use of the library—their children or a friend. (Selected by 16 percent of the respondents.)

- *Patrons* are individuals with a strong sense of belonging to the library. They belong to the Friends group and will often volunteer for the library. (Selected by 16 percent of the respondents.)

- *Scholars* have a deep interest in and a history of research work on one topic area, such as genealogy or religion. (Selected by 9 percent of the respondents.)

- *Spiritual pilgrims* will focus on the library as a place of reflection or rejuvenation. (Selected by 8 percent of the respondents.)

- *Hobbyists* are individuals looking to further their interest in a particular area. (Selected by 4 percent of the respondents.)

- The category *Other* includes those individuals who do not fit into one of the above groups—for example, they are there to drop something off or pick up something. In some communities, this would include the homeless, who are looking for a place to hang out and perhaps use e-mail.

In Singapore, the data collected from a survey of the country's population were subjected to a cluster analysis (a statistical analysis technique), and seven segments with distinct learning- and reading-related lifestyles were identified:[9]

- *The career minded* hold strong beliefs regarding education and family and turn to the library first for their reading.

- *The active information seekers* possess a moderate education, have an entrepreneurial spirit, and place greater importance on social status and material well-being.

- *The self-suppliers* prefer to purchase their own books, are better educated, and hold managerial or executive positions.

- *The group readers* have an avid appetite for reading and are heavy library users.

- *The narrowly focused learners* are students who read to fulfill a course requirement.

- *The low motivators* have little interest in reading.

- *The facilitators* are females with lower education levels who value highly the importance of the library for their children.

As shown in Figure 3.2, identification of the reasons for using the library leads to insights about reading habits and visits to the library.

The benefit segmentation approach has the possibility of significantly improving library services. How would (could) a library organize its services (other than as they are currently organized) to better meet the needs of each benefit segment?

The answer lies in developing a clear picture of each customer group based on benefit segmentation rather than socioeconomic characteristics, so that the library better understands its needs and how the library can add value. Rather than considering the value proposition from a broad perspective, it will be better to try to understand why different benefit segment groups value and use the library. So the question becomes, "What is your library's unique value proposition for each group?" Why does each group use the library rather than going to a bookstore, spending time online seeking information from a search engine, and so forth?

Another related technique that can be used either separately or in conjunction with benefit segmentation groups is to develop personas. A *persona* is a hypothetical representation of a natural grouping of people who drive decision making for a project. Although a persona is not a real person, it does represent real people with unique needs. A persona focuses on what is valuable to that group and their goals when they visit a library. Personas provide a means to understand both existing customers' and noncustomers' expectations of the library's services and products.

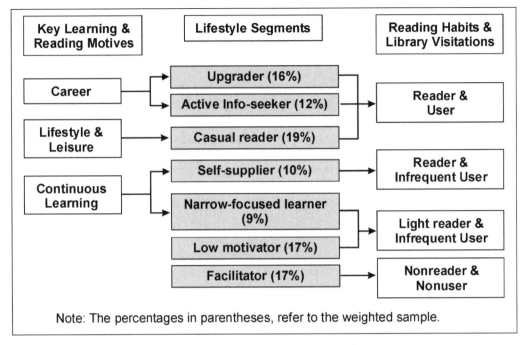

Note: The percentages in parentheses, refer to the weighted sample.

Figure 3.2. Summary Findings of the Seven Segments

Personas are developed not by using customer surveys but rather by involving a number of people in talking about various themes and values. These conversations are recorded and subsequently analyzed. In a project funded by SirsiDynix,[10] seven personas were developed in a public library setting:

Discovery Dan—representing the adult nonresearcher population

Haley High School—representing the high school student population

Jennifer—representing the parents of teenagers

Mommy Marcie—representing the parents of young children

Rick Researcher—representing adult researchers who own a personal computer

Senior Sally—representing senior citizens

Tasha Learner—representing adult researchers who do not own a personal computer

For each of the seven personas, a profile was developed that explored

a typical day at the library,

the group's information-seeking behavior,

their ultimate goal, and

their frustrations.

A sample persona is shown in Figure 3.3 (p. 18).

A typical day at the library: Mother and children typically drive to the library. The four-year-old girl is in a reading group. The two-year-old attends storytelling. Each Monday they go to the library to attend the reading group and to hear a story. Afterward they use the time to check out new books, videos, or DVDs for children, as well as to find time to look for any adult materials.

Information-seeking behavior: The mother typically doesn't have time to use the computer at the library. At the library she is usually busy looking after the children, either participating in a reading group session or attending a storytelling session. She uses the computer at home to put materials on reserve for herself or for the kids if she knows exactly what she wants for them. She picks up the books, DVDs, or videos when she is leaving the library. She uses the library Web site to find out more about upcoming events.

Ultimate goal: The mother wants her children to learn to read and to discover new ideas in a safe, informed setting. She wants her children to be exposed to books early on, even when they don't know how to read yet. She wants to be able to find time to meet some of her own needs, knowing her children are safe.

Frustrations: Not finding librarians who can help the children to learn to read, reduced library hours (nights and weekends), and difficulty finding out about upcoming events on the Web site.

Figure 3.3. Sample Persona: Mommie Marcie. Provided by SirsiDynix.

The consulting firm MAYA Design was part of a team that designed a new library experience for several buildings that were remodeled for the Carnegie Library of Pittsburgh.[11] They observed and interviewed a large group of users and used eight categories of customers to better understand the needs of each group:

Nonuser

Searcher

Learner

Media guy

Explorer

Teen

Parent

Senior

Once the various benefit segments have been identified using interviews as a way to determine why people are using the library, it is possible to conduct a brief survey asking members of each group to rate the importance of various library services and identify the frustrations that they experience when attempting to use the service. The results can then be plotted to show the importance of these services, as shown in Figure 3.4. Michael Magoolaghan, a board member of a small public library in Media, Pennsylvania, demonstrates that the same information architecture used in some projects can also be applied to a small library.[12]

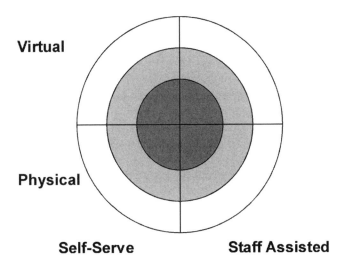

Figure 3.4 Library Customer Activities

The inner circle represents the core or most important library functions or activities, from the perspective of the customer. The middle circle represents supporting activities, and the outer circle represents the peripheral activities. The core activities might be the selection and borrowing of books, picture books, DVDs, and CDs, and attending programs. Supporting activities might be doing research for school, business, or personal lives, and reading magazines or newspapers. Peripheral activities might be to meet friends, surf the Internet/check e-mail, attend meetings, hang out with friends, and so forth. The frequency with which an activity is mentioned in the survey determines its place in the circles.

ADDING VALUE

Regardless of the market segment, the primary challenge for a library is to determine the value proposition for the customer to use the library—physically and virtually. One helpful process is to consider Maslow's hierarchy of needs—physiological, safety, social/belong, esteem, and self-actualization—in the context of delivering valuable services to a library's customer. As shown in Figure 3.5 (p. 20), these five needs can be collapsed when considering the context of the library delivering services.

At the lowest levels, customers are concerned about a clean and comfortable library as well as a well-lit parking lot and building so that their sense of safety is assured. At the next level up, customers are going to be successful—they find the materials they are interested in and they are greeted by name by library staff. And at the top, customers are going to be surprised and delighted by a transformational experience.

In my view, it is crucial to remember that the library must *earn* the customer by somehow *improving the quality of life* of that customer! And what is going to improve the quality of life for each market segment is going to vary. Once the library has earned a customer, you want that customer to (a) keep on coming back and (b) recruit other customers for you. Your purpose then is to create *unique* and *compelling* value for your customers.

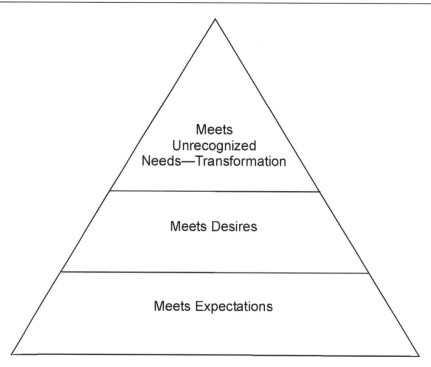

Figure 3.5. The Customer Pyramid. Adapted from Pao-Long Chang and Pao-Nuan Hsieh, "Customer Involvement with Services in Public Libraries," *Asian Libraries* 6, no. 3/4 (1997): 242–49.

The quality of a library service is not what the library puts into it, but rather what the customer receives from it! So focus on what matters—customers. Customers and how they derive benefits should be central to every discussion about the library and its service offerings. The goal is to provide so much value that customers will be thrilled and want to share their WOW experiences with others. Accumulate enough of these delighted customers, and the library's funding decision makers will begin to hear some consistent and very positive messages about the library.

Growing your customer base and making your existing customers come back more frequently is the result of creating real value for them in their daily lives. And these delighted customers will—on their own—recommend the library to their peers and friends. This is what a library should be focused on today and every day in the future.

This is the foundation upon which every successful organization is based. Find your purpose. Find your place. Focus on what truly matters, on what you can have an impact on and what will ultimately ensure your reputation in your community. Turn away from the distractions and noise. Focus on customer value! To do that you must really listen to the "voice of the customer."

CHALLENGE

Consider each of the following benefit segment groups and how the library likely adds value for them, using the groups developed in the study conducted at the Dover Public Library. It might be interesting to see whether each benefit segment group has similar learning styles—visual learners, auditory learners, kinesthetic learners, and so forth. If this were the case, it would be possible for a library to design a set of services that would be more responsive to each benefit segment group.

• *Experience seekers* are looking for activities in the library that will provide entertainment or social connection. These individuals visit the library with the express desire to attend an event (a program, a movie, a book discussion group, an author's talk, etc.).

How the library can add value: In addition to organizing events that will attract the experience seeker, the library can add value by providing links to resources available in the library and online that are related to the event or topic. Some libraries distribute pathfinders and develop displays of library materials that help link library resources, to make the total experience more meaningful and thought provoking. In some cases, the display of library materials is rolled into the room where the program is occurring to encourage browsing and borrowing. You might establish a blog to encourage user involvement and discussion both before and after the event. This would emphasize the role of the library as connector rather than provider—the library can facilitate connections among individuals who have expertise and/or interest in the same topic.

An important question: What else might a library do to add value for this group of library customers?

• *Explorers* are individuals who are curious and love to learn but do not have a specific topic or subject agenda prior to the visit.

How the library can add value: With no specific topic or subject in mind, these individuals would find it helpful to be able to browse the collection. Even if this group were directed to a broad range of Dewey call numbers, implicit in this traditional library response is that the individual knows he or she wants something related to cooking or gardening or . . . Yet the explorer comes to the library with no specific topic in mind. Thus, merchandising the library's collection using face-out displays of materials might have real appeal for this group. Alternatively, it might be possible to organize the library's collection in another unique manner. These customers are more likely to attend programs and classes on any topic and tend to subscribe to newsletters on upcoming events.

In addition, a library might group all material types—books, magazines, DVDs, CDs, and so forth—around a specific topic such as cooking, home improvement, travel, and so forth. This approach has been successfully employed by a number of large bookstores.

An important question: What else might a library do to add value for this group of library customers?

• *Problem solvers*, not surprisingly, are seeking answers to a specific question or problem. Historically libraries have provided access to the library's catalog as a means of opening a door to its collection of materials. It is hoped that these materials will provide answers to the problem solvers questions. In addition, libraries have provided reference services in which reference librarians (and in some cases, other library staff members) are situated behind a service desk. The individual must find the reference service desk and then ask the librarian for assistance. In some cases the individual is directed to (or shown) a specialized collection of reference materials, usually located near the service desk. The assumption is often made that the customer is able to figure out how to use and gain access to the information found in the directory, index, anthology, and so forth.

How the library can add value: Clearly some of the problem solvers who visit are able to navigate in the library and find the resources that provide the answers they are seeking. How large this "self-serve" group of problem solvers is, is unknown. Others will approach a staff member or a service desk. Joan Frye Williams has suggested that an alternative model for providing "research" services is needed in which a nonprofessional staff member performs the "intake" function at the service desk.[13] This individual is trained to link the problem solver with the most appropriate professional librarian, who will assist the customer in finding the answers he or she is seeking. Rather than providing traditional reference services, the librarian is helping the problem solver "research" a question. Thus, they form a team (the customer and the librarian) who work together to solve the problem. Twenty-four-hour chat and instant messaging also help to provide answers at the time of need.

An important question: What else might a library do to add value for this group of library customers?

- *Facilitators* are individuals who are there to support someone else in using the library, such as their children or friends. A facilitator is typically not seeking materials for his or her own use but is at the library to help another to find material of interest. Note that the facilitator may be at the library without the child or friend; he or she might be there to find several books or DVDs that would be of interest to someone who is working or homebound. The facilitator might be a mom or dad helping a child select picture books or attending a children's story hour.

  How the library can add value: Rather than requiring someone to physically visit the library, some libraries offer a service whereby a book, DVD, or other item of interest is mailed directly to the customer's home. The cost of this service might be absorbed by the library's budget, or there might be a small charge to cover the costs of shipping. Some libraries print catalogs of new items in the library's collection and mail them on a quarterly basis to all residents in the jurisdiction. Some libraries distribute e-mails monthly or use an RSS feed indicating what has been recently added to the collection. Some libraries open their doors early for special groups, for example homeschoolers, so staff can devote extra time to ensuring the needs of each individual are met.

  An important question: What else might a library do to add value for this group of library customers?

- *Patrons* are individuals who feel that they belong to the library and that the library is "theirs." These individuals typically belong to the Friends of the Library group and will often volunteer their time to the library.

  How the library can add value: Just as Starbucks, the airlines, hotels, and others offer loyalty cards, perhaps the library should be offering something of value for its patrons. Library patrons could be invited to special VIP events, be given limited editions of a library bag, be given a gold or platinum version of a library card, be able to use the library during special VIP hours, and so forth.

  An important question: What else might a library do to add value for this group of library customers?

- *Scholars* visit the library, physically or virtually, to perform research work in one topic area. Historically, libraries have done a good job of providing a physical setting and a set of finding tools and services that are designed to facilitate research. Yet the library's primary finding tool, the online catalog, is frustrating for many customers to use.

  How the library can add value: As more and more material is being digitized and made accessible via the Internet, the library must begin to explore new ways of delivering research services. In addition to digitizing the local library's special collections, for example, local history, the library must also begin to provide a better set of tools for finding and using this digitized information.

   An important question: What else might a library do to add value for this group of library customers?

- *Spiritual pilgrims* consider the library a place for reflection or rejuvenation. These individuals value quiet study areas so that they can read, reflect, and contemplate the content of a book or other resource. They also value the opportunity to meet like-minded individuals through a book club discussion group.

   How the library can add value: Spiritual pilgrims may be interested in meeting socially with like-minded individuals to explore a topic together.

   An important question: What else might a library do to add value for this group of library customers?

- *Hobbyists* are looking to further their interest in a particular area. The hobbyist is typically seeking up-to-date information about a specific topic. The hobbyist might be interested in finance, cooking, gardening, coin collecting, fly fishing, do-it-yourself home improvement, and so forth.

   How the library can add value: The library might consider partnering with other hobbyist-oriented organizations (cooking clubs, gardening clubs, model train clubs, etc.) in the community to present programs and other activities at the library.

   An important question: What else might a library do to add value for this group of library customers?

It is also important to recognize that an individual might be a part of one benefit segmentation group for some period of time before moving to another. Another individual might move from one group to another the next day, depending on the reason for visiting the library

ACTION PLAN

Create categories of different customer segments. Explore the ways in which needs differ depending on how the library is used (remember the previous discussion of benefit segmentation). What would be a meaningful segmentation for your library that would separate customers with different needs, who would thus use the library and its services in different ways?

Write down what you think you know about your customers. The written descriptions should be created for each customer segment. Describe the primary use of the library for that segment, identify its needs and the reasons those customers use or don't use the library. Don't be surprised that you have difficulty in distinguishing between "wants" and "needs." Remember that you are recording your opinions, so you should not be seeking data about your customers at this stage.

Now consider what you think you know about each customer segment but aren't really sure about. Consider the services and products provided by the library for each group and why you think, but are not sure, they might be using the library. How might your picture of each customer segment be improved if you had access to data? Get out of the library and visit people where they congregate—Starbucks, grocery stores, laundromats, gyms, and so forth.

Get others in your library involved. Ask others to expand the word picture you have been painting about each customer segment. What insights might they have that would paint a clearer and more detailed customer picture? What could others contribute about the needs and customer behavior that you have inadvertently ignored or not considered? Ask others to add to your written descriptions and then share these expanded customer pictures with even more staff members. This iterative process will help construct a more robust picture of each customer segment and how the library adds value from the perspective of the customer.

Begin to compare your word pictures of customer segments with data. Do available socioeconomic and life style data agree with your word pictures? What do the data from the library's integrated library system (ILS) reveal about each customer segment? Is it possible to deduce the reasons different customer segments use the library and the value they derive from each use? Can you infer the value the library brings to the lives of each customer segment?

To complete the word picture for each customer segment, the library may need to organize and conduct a number of focus groups to gain a deeper understanding of the customers, their needs, and their perceptions of your library and its services. The idea is to gain this deep understanding by involving many people rather than relying on our own perceptions, views, and opinions.

Remember that these word pictures of each customer segment, in an outside-in discipline, will identify their needs and behaviors. With this in mind, the library will have the opportunity to consider alternative ways in which to provide a service. These alternatives are called strategies and are considered in much more detail in subsequent chapters of this book.

CONCLUSION

The important point to remember about reinventing the library from the outside-in is that the sole focus is on the customer. What do different customer groups want, and how can the library deliver what the customer needs? Organizations that really do well spend a lot of time listening, and in particular they listen to the "voice of the customer."

The library will need to redesign and reengineer its services using customer-driven empathic design that leads to "WOW" moments. This probably means going beyond customer-expressed needs so that your understanding of a customer segment is so deep you are able to discern needs that the customer has not expressed. Getting close to the customer is not really a new concept. Tom Peters and Bob Waterman, in *In Search of Excellence*, suggest that this was one of their key findings about innovative companies.[14]

The goal is to **WOW** customers by attuning the library's services and offerings in ways that will help them experience dimensions of delight that normally are not achieved (and most likely, were previously unknown!). The customers are so delighted with the new library experience that they will want to share it with their friends, neighbors, and coworkers—in short, with everyone they encounter!

NOTES

1. *The Mind of the Strategist: The Art of Japanese Business* (New York: McGraw-Hill, 1991).

2. For an example of how this approach might work in your library, see Marc Futterman, "Finding the Underserved," *Library Journal* 133, no. 17 (October 15, 200): 42–45.

3. These and other related studies are discussed and summarized in chapter 7 of Joseph R. Matthews, *The Evaluation and Measurement of Library Services* (Westport, CT: Libraries Unlimited, 2007).

4. Joseph R. Matthews, "Customer Satisfaction: A New Perspective," *Public Libraries* (November/ December 2008).

5. Joan Frye Williams, conversation with author, n.d.

6. Akio Sone, "An Application of Discrete Choice Analysis to the Modeling of Public Library Use and Choice Behavior," *Library & Information Science Research* 10 (1988): 35–55.

7. Referenced in Pao-Long Chang and Pao-Nuan Hsieh, "Customer Involvement with Services in Public Libraries," *Asian Libraries* 6, nos. 3/4 (1997): 242–49. Text in Chinese.

8. Institute for Learning Innovation, *Dover, DE Library User Identity—Motivation Pilot Study* (Dover: Delaware Division of Libraries, December 2005). The study used a convenience sample size of 113 one-on-one interviews.

9. Kau Ah Keng, Kwon Jung, and Jochen Wirtz, "Segmentation of Library Visitors in Singapore: Learning and Reading Related Lifestyles," *Library Management* 24, nos. 1/2 (2003): 20–33.

10. Mary Lee Kennedy, "The Library as the User Sees It," *SirsiDynix One Source* 2, no. 8 (August 2006). Available at www.imakenews.com/sirsi/e_article000627222.cfm?x=b11,0,w.

11. You can learn more about MAYA and its involvement with the Carnegie Library of Pittsburgh at /www.maya.com/portfolio/carnegie-library

12. Michael Magoolaghan, "Redesigning the Library Experience," *Bulletin of the American Society for Information Science & Technology* 34, no. 7 (October/November 2008): 41–43.

13. Williams, n.d.

14. Thomas Peters and Robert Waterman, *In Search of Excellence: Lessons from America's Best-run Companies* (New York: Warner, 1982).

4

Library as Place

The idea of the library has always been bigger than the building itself, which is a necessary and convenient place for storing things. It also makes a great meeting place, touchstone for the community, and symbol for the values we share and uphold. The building stands for something, and we should be proud of the places it occupies in the minds of our clienteles.

—Joseph James[1]

Public libraries have been built on a central ideal: to make available shared (principally print-based) resources that can be used by all members of the community to stimulate imagination and inquiry and nuture the development of culture and commerce. Libraries offer a range of products and services that are open to all and, it is hoped, will benefit those who are least able to afford purchasing similar services. It is the combination of community and choice, provided by publicly supported funding for private benefit, that makes the concept of the public library so special.

One of the clear challenges facing a library in any community is where to locate it and, at some point as the size of the community grows, where to place additional library facilities. A plethora of studies has examined the importance of distance as a factor in determining use of a library. The principal conclusion of these studies is that the impact of distance is not a simple and constant factor; rather, that impact is influenced by the socioeconomic status of the community, the age of the residents, and the characteristics of the library itself and any barriers to access that naturally occur, for example, a river, a freeway, and so forth. The use of a library by children is clearly affected by distance (i.e., the closer a child lives to a library, the more likely he or she is to use it), whereas an adult is willing to travel farther (especially if the library is "appealing" for some reason).

For many people, safety and "ease of use" are really what drives the decision to visit a particular organization. Saving the customer's time should be one of the driving forces behind any library's decision to reinvent itself from the

outside-in!

27

In medium- and large-sized communities, the assumption is often made that a central or main library building is needed. This ignores two very important and fundamental questions that should be asked. First, is a central library really needed? The answer will depend on the needs of the community being served. In addition, it is important to recognize that the library does not exist in a vacuum. Some communities are surrounded by good public libraries that are located in other jurisdictions, as well as one or more large academic institutions. For example, citizens living in the San Francisco Bay area live in a "library-rich environment," with a number of large public and academic libraries to choose from. So the need for a central library must be carefully considered. Second, if a central library is needed, then what are the roles and responsibilities of the main library compared to the role of the branches?

An obvious question that arises about the need to build one or more branch libraries is what kind of branch library should be built. There are two general options:

A "full-service" branch

A specialized branch

A full-service branch library will offer almost all of the services found in a main library, except that the building, collections, and staff levels are smaller. A specialized branch will focus on meeting the needs of a niche market segment and will exclude all nonrelevant library services. Each of these options is discussed in greater detail below.

FULL-SERVICE BRANCH LIBRARIES

Branch libraries, called extension agencies more than a hundred years ago, were typically viewed as distributing agencies and as advertising for the main library, making the resources of the main library known to the neighborhood community. Librarians felt that no branch facility should ever consider itself a substitute for the main library. They hoped that use of the neighborhood branch library would encourage people to travel to the distant main library.

This situation began to change in the 1940s, starting with a landmark study of the Chicago Public Library by Carleton Joeckel and Leon Carnovsky, who were faculty members of the Graduate Library School at the University of Chicago. They suggested that the library system expand the number and the variety of services offered in a branch library.[2] The authors found that a vast majority of the customers relied solely on the resources and services of the neighborhood branch library, and few used the branch as a stepping stone to the main library.

Lowell Martin, one of the library profession's preeminent public library planning and building consultants, completed his master's thesis in 1940. His thesis advisors, not surprisingly, were Carleton Joeckel and Leon Carnovsky. Martin's thesis was the foundation upon which he developed a series of ideas and recommendations that were included in a major planning studies done for many large library systems over the course of the next 40 years.[3] Following are the continuing themes reflected in these planning reports:

- **The need for three levels of library facilities**—smaller neighborhood branches, larger regional libraries, and a main or central library. The branch library was to serve a local clientele, whose reading demands were limited in scope. Regional libraries provide access to a broader range of materials and services. The central library was to house the largest collection and act as a community "research" library.

- **Branch libraries have a different mission** than the main library and should be treated as discrete units, with very specific collections, services, and facilities designed to meet the needs of the local community. Branch library collections should focus on high-demand materials and not attempt to provide a "well rounded" collection.

- The belief that **libraries should be providing access to audiovisual materials**.

- The idea that **books and other materials in branch libraries should be organized in an "interest arrangement"** rather than by one of the more traditional classification schemes (Dewey or Library of Congress call numbers). The intent of the subject interest grouping of materials is to provide good (recent) books and then "draw the visitor's attention to them." This sounds very similar to merchandising a library's collection! Martin suggested using a series of broad subject groupings of nonfiction books, disregarding classification numbers. Fiction materials could also be organized by categories for readers seeking diversion and recreation. Unfortunately this idea did not gain much traction.

Despite these studies, most library systems have created branch library facilities that provide much of what also can be found in a main library (given building space constraints):

A children's collection featuring numerous picture books

An area to hold children's story hours

A popular adult fiction collection

A nonfiction collection

An audiovisual (media) collection

A reference desk staffed by one or more reference librarians

A print reference collection

A number of computers that provide Internet access

A meeting room

The usual collection of tables and chairs

A circulation desk

In almost all cases, every branch library is treated as all others are (making adjustments for size). Thus, new materials are allocated on a formula basis to all branches in the name of equality, without regard to the fact that some portions of the collection are more heavily used than others in one branch than in another. The needs and interests of a neighborhood surrounding a branch are different, but this is typically not recognized when planning library collections and services. The goal for most libraries is to provide a "balanced" collection, with some material on most subjects, waiting on the shelves for the possible user.

It is clear that a very important part of planning for branch library facilities is to have a clear and explicit statement about the role of the branch library. Simply acknowledging financial realities will suggest that most branch libraries should provide greater access to a collection of physical materials and services that are specifically targeted to meet the particular needs of the community in which they are located rather than attempting to provide a "balanced" collection.

A report prepared by the Urban Libraries Council discussed the efforts of the Chicago Public Library to foster branch libraries so that the library is at the center of the local community's life.[4] A library can serve as an anchor for neighborhoods and communities. The libraries accomplished this by reaching out and building a bridge to the community, engaging with key individuals and partnering with other community organizations. The branch collections are reflective of the interests and languages spoken in the local community. Collaborating with other organizations has resulted in the development of innovative programs such as financial literacy classes and free children's passes to museums. The key to such a strategy is to ensure that branch librarians and other staff members have outgoing personalities, so that they really like engaging with members of the community.

Given that the vast majority of branch libraries are all very similar in terms of collections and services provided, it is quite clear that most librarians, library building consultants, and architects have assumed

Traditional libraries reach traditional users. Nontraditional libraries reach everybody.
—Michelle Gorman[5]

that all new branch libraries should also be similar. However, it is possible to consider other options for a branch library.

UNIQUE OR NARROWLY FOCUSED LIBRARIES

One option for a branch library is to be narrowly focused and designed to meet the needs of a specific segment of the population. The library will go through the process of identifying different market segments that it has and has not been serving and will know what type of unique library would fit in the community. Public libraries in Asia, Europe, and South America have been designing and building unique libraries. These unique libraries have been described as "niche libraries," "boutique libraries," and "lifestyle libraries."

The National Library Board in Singapore is responsible for the operation of all public libraries, community college libraries, government agency libraries, and one university library. In 2000 the National Library Board began transforming itself by reinventing libraries from the outside-in. The mission for the library is to expand the learning capacity of the nation. The service vision is to deliver services that are convenient, accessible, affordable, and useful. The transformation focused on four building blocks: content, services, people, and infrastructure.

The public libraries in Singapore used the transformation opportunity to prototype new facilities and services rather than relying on "plain vanilla" libraries. These test beds allowed staff to improve on the prototypes, and the successful ideas and concepts were then incorporated into new buildings and rolled out to existing branches.

The library system has 23 library facilities. The use of these facilities in Singapore jumped substantially from 2000 to 2006: annual visits increased from 5.7 million to 38 million; circulation went from 10 million to 29 million; and inquiries multiplied, from 50,000 to 2.8 million. At the same time, the average age of the collections has decreased, from 11.5 years to less than 5 years![6]

Like many library systems in the states, Singapore has built three very large regional libraries—about 120,000 square feet in size—that contain a collection of some 500,000 items. Each regional library has four floors, each of which is targeted to a different market segment—reference, children, young adult (with large study areas), and adult. Circulation in each of these libraries runs more than two million items annually.

Community Children's Library

At one time Singapore had some 30 community children's libraries (there currently are two), which are fairly small—about 2,500 square feet—and specifically designed for children aged four to ten. Everything is designed for these small "customers" including the furniture, the collection, and services. There are multiple copies of popular picture books to assist young children in learning to read. There are lots of story times offered during the morning, afternoon, and evening. In short, it's a "small world library" for small children. Cool!

In Singapore, the target market for a children's library is a large housing complex. The community provides the space, and volunteers to help run the library—a volunteer must be present for the library to be open. The library provides part-time staff for story hours, library materials, self-checkout/return machines, and maintenance of the facility.

Another wonderful children's library is the Library of Picture Books in Iwaki City in Fukushima Prefecture in Japan. This is a bright and airy building with open bookshelves on every wall, featuring face-out picture books. The building provides various flights of stairs, which gives children the opportunity to find a space to withdraw and read or to interact with other children.

Adult Community Library

An adult community library serves the adults of a local community, providing popular fiction, nonfiction, and audiovisual materials. The library does not provide children's services. Customers who need reference service use a kiosk that provides an audio and visual link to a reference librarian located in one of the larger regional libraries. The kiosk includes a printer so the customer can leave with a record of the assistance provided, if needed.

Shopping Mall Library

In Singapore, the shopping mall libraries are located in the key regional shopping malls of the country and are focused on the young adult segment of the population. These libraries are modest in size, roughly 16,000 square feet, and their collections are primarily audiovisual, with a small collection of popular magazines. The appeal of these shopping mall libraries is undeniable: They account for about 40 percent of circulation and attendance (gate count), yet they are less than 20 percent of the total public library space.[7]

These shopping mall libraries even have appealing names—Library@Orchard (Orchard Road is the busiest shopping street in Singapore), Library@CompassPoint, Library@Esplanade (a performing arts complex), and so forth. In 2009 the National Library Board was looking for new space for the Library@Orchard because its lease had expired.

The Experience Library

The Cerritos (CA) library has created an "Experience Library" in a large, 88,500-square-foot facility that houses some 300,000 books. This three-story building offers a rich experience for any visitor, including a 15,000-gallon saltwater aquarium at the entrance to the unique multimedia learning centers, as well as "themed" spaces to define its different collections. An Old World Reading Room, with its wood paneling and a fireplace, provides access to rare first editions, unique collectible books, and new and popular titles. A World Traditions area recognizes the contributions of non-Western cultures to society with a special collection of print and multimedia resources in languages other than English and in non-Roman alphabets.

The Children's Library has a "Save the Planet" theme that aims to stimulate a sense of discovery with a variety of specially designed exhibits and artifacts, including a full-sized replica of a *Tyrannosaurus rex* fossil, a scale-model of a NASA space shuttle, a lighthouse, an arts studio, and a Little Theater. An Art Deco area provides access to a rich array of multimedia resources.

"InfoStations" extend customer service to points throughout the building. Modeled after a hotel concierge desk, the stations provide quick assistance of a general or directional nature. Librarians and computer technicians with wireless headsets roam the floor providing hands-on assistance to users.

Electronic resources include some 200 computer workstations, 1,200 laptop ports, wireless access, and a state-of-the-art computer lab. Multimedia learning centers integrate print materials with Web resources and computer graphics. This is a library that simply hums with excitement and energy.

Idea Stores

Tower Hamlets is a disadvantaged inner borough comprising most of London's East End and is characterized by high unemployment, low education levels, poor job skills, and a diverse population (more than 50 languages are spoken in the borough). Use of the public libraries in this area had fallen quite dramatically.

Working closely with the community and using a variety of methods to seek their views and opinions about their needs and how the public library could become more relevant in their lives, the library reached a surprising conclusion. Reinvent the library! A partnership with the borough's Office of Lifelong Learning Services was formed to combine adult and recreational education with traditional library functions.

Feedback from the community also suggested that the brand "library" conveyed the feeling of old, crumbling, and irrelevant, and an "institutional feel" that did not resonate with the community members. Thus was born the concept of a new brand—The Idea Store! The Tower Hamlets are building a total of seven Idea Stores. The modern facilities are flexible in design and permit the integration of educational, community, and library services. Each Idea Store provides meeting rooms, classrooms, computer labs, books, and audiovisual collections. Rooms have glass walls and other partitions that can be moved. A café is provided to encourage people to relax, read, and chat.

The Idea Stores are located near major retail establishments, and large windows allow those passing by to observe the activities inside. The idea is to place the Idea Stores where the street life of the local community is today, not where it was a hundred years ago. By the end of 2008 four Idea Stores had been opened. The interiors are bright, and shelving is little more than waist high, to facilitate wayfinding within the building.[8] Use of the Idea Stores is quite high (based on the number of people who enter an Idea Store each year), whereas annual circulation is quite low, which is not surprising because the collections are quite small.

DOK

The DOK, located in the city of Delft in the Netherlands, is a media center that combines three collections: music and film ("Discotake" in Dutch), literature ("Openbare Bibliotheek") , and art ("Kunstcentrum"). These three collections, together with the expertise of the staff, form the foundation for the flow of creativity and energy of the individuals who visit the DOK. The attraction of the DOK is emphasized by the fact that more than 500,000 people visit the library each year and must purchase an annual membership card.

The DOK has set the bar quite high when it comes to its mission: to become and remain the most advanced library in the world. The DOK "endeavors to be an indispensable source of inspiration for its members, visitors and partners in the city of Delft."[9] Recognizing that the world is changing rapidly and that the Internet is making walls and boundaries disappear, the focus of the DOK is to keep, make, and share stories, regardless of the medium. To keep up with developments in the world and maintain its high level of service to its customers, the library sent out three librarians for a three-week tour of the United States. These "Shanachies" (Irish for storyteller) traveled more than 5,000 miles, gathering and telling stories.

The DOK created a mobile studio with cameras, sound systems, and editing software to make documentaries and do videocasts. DOK staff visit high schools, where students are encouraged to write scripts and create films on a variety of topics. On their trip to the United States, the Shanachies created a video titled *If You're Not Gaming, You're Losing*. During their visits to several libraries that actively promoted gaming among teens, they found that book circulation increased by 70 percent among teens. The DOK also partners with a children's day care center and developed a summer camp.

In May 2007 the DOK opened its new building, which provides a colorful and aesthetically pleasing library—in short, *a destination*. Graphics on banners are colorful and attractive, and natural language names are used to identify collections rather than a call number range. Comfortable furniture is provided, and the goal is to encourage each visitor to have fun! Flexibility in this new building is a central design element—for example, shelving is mounted on casters so that it can be moved to create space for activities. Recently the library began experimenting with digital download stations, both in the library and at several locations around town. The idea is to download library digital content to mobile phones and other personal digital devices.

Because the shelving is on wheels, it can be moved off to the sides of rooms when large events are held in the library. Staff can rearrange the shelving to enable a better "flow" or help users find something more easily. The shelving is also shorter than shelving in most libraries. This eliminates the feeling that the library shelving is about to "close in on you."

CONVERGENCE

Convergence involves co-locating individual cultural facilities, for example, a library and a museum, in one location. It also involves sharing staffing, programming, and other services in new and creative ways.

One of the challenges of the concept of convergence is that a new concept of space in museums and libraries is needed. Historically exhibition space was very carefully structured to minimize contact and interaction with the exhibit materials. More recently, some museums have been experimenting with ways to encourage more interaction among and between the exhibit and those in the building or viewing the exhibit via the Internet.

The goal is to find ways of integrating exhibits and library materials that will surprise and delight visitors. This is no small task, because once the novelty has worn off, these integrated elements will occupy space but nay not be used by the local community in any meaningful manner. It also requires the staff from each institution to learn new skills and be cross trained.

Convergence has occurred at the Tamworth Regional Gallery & Library, the Manly Gallery & Museum, the Albury City Library/Museum, the Puke Ariki Library/Museum, the Tamworth Library & Art Gallery, the Wanneroo Library & Heritage Services (all located in Australia), and in New Plymouth, New Zealand. Some of these communities have merged facilities and staff; others are sharing space while staff remain separate.

ADDING UNIQUE FUNCTIONS/ACTIVITIES IN A LIBRARY

ImaginOn is a joint venture of the Public Library of Charlotte & Mecklenburg County and the Children's Theatre of Charlotte, which built a combined children's library and theater. The mission of ImaginOn is to "bring stories to life through extraordinary experiences that challenge, inspire and excite young minds"—in short, *a place to have fun!* The Story Lab provides individual workstations called Tale Spinners as well as a podlike arrangement of computers called Team Machines. The computers are magical purple and yellow in color, with spiraling turrets and pipes that lead to unknown places. Young people use these computers with software that challenges them to expand their imaginations while writing stores. Stories can be added to the Story Jar for others to discover.

ImaginOn is housed in a 102,000-square-foot facility that cost about $42 million to construct. Wayfinding within ImaginOn is intuitive: light, sight, and color are used effectively. One of the popular destinations in the building is Tech Central, which provides 40 computers for tweens. A five-person staff is available to assist the children to learn how to use the software and write more effective stories. An additional 15 computers are provided in a classroom setting for children to learn how to do research and learn fairly sophisticated software, such as Dreamweaver and PowerPoint. This hands-on approach to learning generates a real buzz among the tweens.

The Loft in ImaginOn is a 4,000-square-foot space designed to attract teenagers by providing oversized booths for teen to work together (Wi-Fi access is provided) or simply hang out. Comfortable chairs are also provided, so that the teens can kick back and relax (and even read a book). A gleaming metal and glass media area presents the work of the teens. Library online services are available via IM (instant messaging).

Adjacent to the Loft is a music and animation studio, called Studio I, which provides animation, video, editing, and music creation capabilities. Cameras, lighting, a blue screen, and whiteboards are available. Teens, and on some days adults too, can use the equipment to create animated and regular videos, which often wind up on YouTube; take pictures to put on Facebook; and play video games such as Rock Band, Guitar Hero, Dance Dance Revolution, and all the Wii sports games. The goal of the Loft is to provide a space that resonates with today's teens and their changing media habits so that the public library does not slide into oblivion.

A Teen Library

The Queens Library created a bright and welcoming teens' library using 3,200 square feet of leased space near its existing branch in Far Rockaway, New York. Lots of comfortable, overstuffed seating is provided, along with several peninsulas to accommodate 40 computers. Chairs, tables, and partitions are on wheels to allow for rearrangement to accommodate various activities. The library is only open during after-school hours.

Less Is More

The Brookdale branch of the Hennepin County Library took another approach. When planning for its remodeling, library staff met with community groups, including a large group of recent immigrants, and local officials and held a series of focus groups. The results suggested that the residents wanted a library that was simpler to use and was more focused on some very specific high-interest areas, including small business, careers, automotive, homework, technology, recreational reading, and little else.

The 53,000-square-foot library, which reopened in 2004, reduced its collection by 50 percent and organized the collection around subject areas called "information neighborhoods." These neighborhoods are marked by large retail-style signs that declare, for example, "Health & Fitness" or "Careers." Each neighborhood has its own unique carpet design so the customers will know they are in a new neighborhood. Each information neighborhood includes all the materials on the subject area—both circulating and reference. The one-stop approach makes things easier for the less-skilled user, which hopefully will translate into a long-term relationship with the library.[10]

The library also provides space for 118 computers with free access to the Internet.

Prototype Library

The Aarhus Public Library in Denmark has developed a project called The Transformation Lab, which is designed to answer the question, "When everything is available online, why come to the library at all?"

Included in the project are the Literature Lab, the Music Lab (which includes an Inspiration Zone), the News Lab, The Square, and the Exhibition Lab. The Lab is located in the main entry of the library and was a collaboration between the library and several other organizations. Most important, it involves the active participation of the customer as a real partner and collaborator. User involvement in possible prototypes is all about "co-creation."

The lessons learned from this series of experiments are that

- flexible spaces are necessary;

- open events are a good idea and well received;

- the physical library needs to be augmented with interactive technology;

- networking is critical among users, IT specialists, library staff, and architects; and

- users need to have a more visible role inside the library.

Not surprisingly, customers like to become involved as long as it is not too much trouble and brings about an instant result. The end result is that people have been forced to dismiss the book as library brand and that through this project they are becoming co-creators of a new library space.

The library has developed a series of videos that document these experiments.[11]

An MDM

The library might consider installing a materials dispensing machine, or MDM—sometimes called a vending jukebox or a book-lending machine. The MDM can hold a fairly large number of books, CDs, DVDs, or some combination of material types, depending on the size of the machine. The machines could be placed in the library itself (to reduce loss of materials) or where people congregate—shopping centers, subway platforms, and so forth. The machines can be set into a wall or built as a stand-alone kiosk. The Contra Costa County Library is the first in America to offer public library book-lending machines. Located at the Bay Area Rapid Transit's (BART) Pittsburg/Bay Point station, Library-a-Go-Go (the MDM) allows commuters with a Contra Costa County (CA) library card convenient access to library books.

Amenities

Coffee shops are now an integral part of many retail stores, and many members of the library community have suggested that a library should provide space for such an amenity. At the Botany Downs Library in New Zealand, customers can purchase a glass of wine to sip while reading a magazine. Such a step calls into question libraries' traditional aversion to allowing food and drink (let alone beer and wine) into a library. This and other amenities can do much to make the library a more welcoming space.

Wayfinding

Many library users find the layout of collections and services to be difficult, confusing, and often intimidating to navigate. Typically staff members are surprised by this and expect a library customer to ask for help (at a service desk), understand the layout of the library, and have plenty of time to enjoy all that the library has to offer! Yet many studies have demonstrated that people, especially men, do not ask for help, do not understand how to use a great many of the tools provided by the library, and typically spend only short periods of time in the library.

First impressions of a library and its usability are important. They ultimately affect whether people will return to the library time and again, because people choose to use services that elicit feelings of comfort and pleasure. Remember that Zipf's Law of Least Effort is alive and well and operates in physical library spaces as well as online. Zipf's Law states that people tend to choose perceived ease of access over quality of content. Frustration levels quickly rise, because most first-time library visitors do not understand library jargon, abbreviations, and acronyms.

Remember that the library has four basic components, as shown in Figure 4.1. These components of the library experience include the following:

- **Customers:** the people who use the library. Remember that they come in many "flavors," and there is no one "typical" customer.

- **Organizers:** the way in which tools and systems organize the materials in a library's collections, including:

    - *Physical space:* the first organizer that people will encounter. This includes the shelving and how it is organized, displays, tables and chairs, signage, size and shape of the service desks, and so forth.

    - *Organizational schemes:* the library's catalog, but also other tools, including how the collection is organized (call number order, broad subjects, or some other method), pathfinders, lists, and so forth.

    - *Librarians* and other staff members, as well as friends of the customers, who may be giving reader assistance advice, directions, or instruction.

- **Materials and services:** the reasons people use the library. This component includes the library collections (physical and electronic) as well as the wide variety of services frequently offered by the library, including story hours, instruction classes, programs, discussions, exhibits, speakers, films, and so forth.

- **Use/Participation:** the actual interaction with the materials and activities in the library or online. The most frequent use is the borrowing of materials (which are then returned), placing a reserve (hold) on an item, attending a program, asking for research assistance, and so forth.

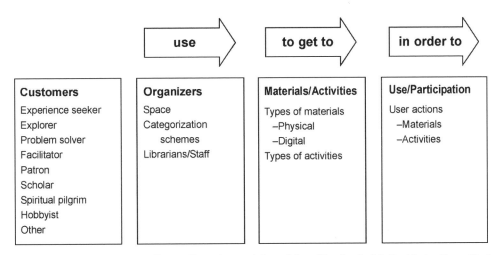

Figure 4.1. Components of the Library Experience. Adapted from Heather L. McQuaid, Aradhana Goel, and Mickey McManus, "When You Can't Talk to Customers: Using Storyboards and Narratives to Elicit Empathy for Users," *DPPI '03 Conference Proceedings* (June 23–26, 2003): 120–25.

Customers have a wide variety of concerns and emotional responses as the result of attempting to use the library, including uncertainty/confusion, fear, anxiety, annoyance, and in some cases, delight and joy.

Libraries must find the means to dramatically improve wayfinding for all users, especially in library buildings that have multiple floors that require reorientation in terms of layout, because individual areas are rarely delimited or visually "marked" in a distinctive manner. This is especially true when various types of materials are stored on shelving that is uniform, despite type of media.

CONCLUSION

Although every community is different (and it is incumbent upon the library to have a clear understanding of the various market segments in a community), it is important to recognize that the library can become *a destination* within a community. However, as evidenced by the abundant examples of the different types of libraries discussed previously, there is no one "right" model for everyone. The cookie cutter is simply not going to work. The reinvented library only works if it meets the needs of the majority of people who live, work, and play in your community.

Clearly the reinvented library has to be designed in collaboration with those for whom it is being built. Thus, it may be that a group of teens, or mothers with small children, or . . . will be active participants in the design process. This will help ensure that the library is being designed from the

outside-in!

As libraries envision new library facilities or plan to remodel existing ones, it is time reinvent themselves to create the customer-focused library—from the **outside-in!** New library buildings need to have less space devoted to storage of materials (traditional shelving) and more space that is flexible.

Libraries have to create a "third" space—neither home nor office, a place where people will want to spend time. A customer-focused library demands a focus on programming, reading, interaction, events, and partnerships with other community groups to make the library a vibrant, important place for the individuals in a community.

NOTES

1. "In the Library," *American Libraries* (June/July 2008): 49.

2. Carleton Joeckel and Leon Carnovsky, *A Metropolitan Library in Action: A Survey of he Chicago Public Library* (Chicago: University of Chicago Press, 1940).

3. Lowell Martin completed a series of planning studies for a number of library systems, including Los Angeles (1949), Baltimore County (1957), Dallas Public Library (1958), Chicago (1968), Philadelphia (1981), and San Francisco (1982), among others.

4. *The Engaged Library: Chicago Stories of Community Building* (Evanston, IL: Urban Libraries Council, 2005).

5. Quoted in Brian Kenney, "Imagine This," *School Library Journal* (December 2005): 55.

6. Statistics are from the Singapore Public Library's annual reports.

7. Christopher Chia, "Transformation of Libraries in Singapore," *Library Review* 50, nos. 7/8 (2001): 343–48.

8. More information about the Idea Store is available at ideastore.co.uk.

9. Erik Boekesteijn, "Discover Innovations at DOK, Holland's 'Library Concept Center'," *Marketing Library Services* 22, no. 2 (March/April 2008): 1–4.

10. Beth Dempsey, "Designing Buildings and Services from the End User's Viewpoint Transforms Access for Everyone," *Library Journal* 130, no. 20 (December 15, 2005): 72–75.

11. The library in Aashus, Denmark, has developed three videos that document their project: Transformation Lab—Prototyping the Future, available at www.youtube.com/watch?v=TpFO_L_jA1c; I-Land, www.youtube.com/watch?v=c1zS_oIPD_0; Story Surfer, and www.youtube.com/watch?v=rW-rrQI06OA.

5

The Library Collection

The library catalog . . . is a place where bibliographic records get lost alphabetically. The library collection . . . is a place where an item gets lost in call number sequence.

Over time a library will invest a significant amount of money in creating and maintaining its collection—both physical and electronic. Despite the fact that the physical collection is sitting on shelving and directly accessible to the library customer, it remains, for the most part, an almost invisible resource. Ezra Schwartz has characterized this as the "iceberg problem."[1] Like an iceberg, most of the collection remains invisible. Even if a customer were to systematically read each title on the spine, he or she would quickly become overwhelmed at the extent of the resources and be unable to really understand what the collection actually contains—even from a broad subject perspective. One of the primary reasons for this iceberg problem is the shelves the library uses to store materials.

Over time, libraries have developed shelving that is very efficient. As the number of shelves increased in height, the density of library materials increased. The books and other materials are stored in a spine-out fashion and are arranged in either call number order or alphabetically by author's last name (for fiction materials). In a lot of libraries, almost all other material types are stored in spine-out fashion using shelving that was originally designed for books. Thus, a customer must search for CDs, videocassettes, DVDs, and other materials looking only at the spine—often needing to ignore a generous collection of labels and stickers—to find the desired item.

One alternative way to organize a library's collection is to use bookstore-type shelving or displays that are designed to merchandise books, DVDs, CDs, and so forth. A number of public libraries have been exploring, to one degree or another, the use of merchandising techniques in their libraries. This desire to adopt an alternative strategy for making library materials available to their customers stems, in part, from the recognition that the "same old, same old" is no longer

[R]aises an important question for librarians: Can a 1.0 collection survive in a 2.0 world?

—Nicole Heintzleman et al.[2]

39

satisfactory and that there has to be a better way to present the library's collection to the community. Given the volume of directional questions in most libraries, clearly many customers don't get that "Dewey Decimal thing."

Recognizing that a majority of library customers do not use the library's online catalog but rather select materials by browsing (most people come to the library without a specific title in mind), some libraries have turned to merchandising as a way to assist customers in their browsing and to find items they otherwise might have overlooked. Although merchandising has proven to be popular with library customers, some in the library profession have characterized and criticized the use of merchandising techniques as an attempt to turn a library into "just another bookstore."

The roots of merchandising can be found in Lowell Martin's master's thesis at the University of Chicago in 1940, in which he recommended the "interest arrangement" of the library's materials rather than Dewey Decimal classification for organizing the collection. Charles Robinson embraced this concept when he was the director of the Baltimore County (MD) Public Library, which transformed branches using bookstore display units. I once had the opportunity of visiting one of these branch libraries with Charlie, and he was delighted when a young mother had browsed the collection, made several choices, then approached the circulation desk, pushed the items across the desk, and asked "How much?" Charlie literally beamed with pride!

MERCHANDISING

Merchandising involves more than simply displaying a portion of the collection face-out on slat walls, tables, and display units. Rather, it is adopting a customer perspective so that the library transforms itself to better deliver its services in ways that are more appealing to a broader segment of the population. Remember that more than half of the people visiting the library will spend less than 15 minutes there!

Merchandising includes such issues such as wayfinding (the layout, signage, and other clues about where things are located in the library), traffic flows of people in the library, lighting, display fixtures and furniture for materials, choice of paint colors, carpeting, comfortable furniture, and so forth. Perhaps most important is that the library may need to rearrange space to provide improved access to the merchandised collection. The Denver Public Library and the Mt. Laurel Public Library in New Jersey have suggested that merchandising is adding WOW to the library.[3] The San Jose Public Library calls areas of the library that have merchandised collections "the marketplace."[4]

Whereas some libraries have added a few display units in their library and consider the result merchandising, others, such as the Denver Public Library, the Markham (Ontario, Canada) Public Library, the Mt. Laurel Public Library, the Richmond (British Columbia, Canada) Public Library, the Brookdale branch of the Hennepin County Library, and the San Jose Public Library have embraced merchandising to a much greater degree. San Jose merchandises (any departure from a strict spine-out, Dewey-ordered shelving method) about 50 percent of its collection in each location. There seems to be a merchandising continuum, from low to high, in the amount of space in a facility that is devoted to merchandising. The whole idea is to make customers comfortable and encourage browsing.

For example, the Brighouse (Main) Branch of the Richmond Public Library (British Columbia, Canada) devotes approximately 75 percent of its available space to merchandising. An example of the "power wall units" used by the Richmond Public Library is shown in Figure 5.1. Notice that each unit has a large graphic sign indicating the focus of the unit and that a majority of the space is devoted to the face-out presentation of library materials. In addition, the display unit provides space for the traditional spine-out display of items (although accessible to the customers and staff, this area serves as a "stockpile" area so that items can be pulled to keep the displays fresh and full).

Figure 5.1. "Power Wall" Units at the Richmond (British Columbia, Canada) Public Library.
Photo by Joe Matthews

Other ways to merchandise the library's collection include items commonly found in most bookstores—multilevel display tables, stand-alone display units (for books, CDs, DVDs), end caps on shelving units, slat walls on the ends of shelving, mixing face-out and spine-out shelving of books, and so forth.

The results of merchandising have been very positive in other libraries. For example, Joan Bernstein, director of the Mt. Laurel (NJ) Public Library, noted that "circulation has doubled in the five years since we introduced merchandising in our library."[5]

The San Jose Public Library, with 17 branches and a main library, has seen its circulation increase over the last 10 years from about 4 million to over 14 million items a year—that's a 350 percent increase!

Clearly when some of the display units are placed in proximity to the circulation area, library customers are more inclined to "grab something that looks interesting." Such behavior is similar to that of people exposed to point-of-purchase displays at local supermarkets or other stores. However, rather than spending money, the library customer is more likely to find an item or two of interest.

ORGANIZING THE DISPLAYS

Merchandising involves more than displaying a library's new books, media, and current interest topics. It involves a new way of browsing the library's fiction and nonfiction collections using topical categories, themes, or subject matter. Examples of such topical themes are Health & Wellness, Home & Garden, How It Works, Computers, Facts & Trivia, True Crime, Crafts & Hobbies, Cars, Bikes & Boats, Chick Lit, Movie Tie-ins, Living Green, Stranger Than Fiction, Books for Dummies, and Self-Help, Pets and Barbeque/Grilling during the Summer. Well, you get the idea.

Large signs above each merchandise unit assist the customer in identifying a category or topic that may be of interest, as illustrated in Figure 5.2. Some libraries have extended the concept of merchandising the entire collection by placing topic signs above each range of shelves, as illustrated in Figure 5.3.

Figure 5.2. Merchandising Signs at the Markham (Ontario, Canada) Public Library.
Photo courtesy of the Markham Public Library

Figure 5.3. Merchandising the Collection.
Photo courtesy of the Markham Public Library

One of the challenges facing a library is selecting a specific range of Dewey call numbers to include in each category. In some cases, i.e., computers, it may be necessary to have two or more call number ranges included in a merchandise category. For example, the Self-Help section would need to include books from the 100s, 300s, and 600s; the Books for Dummies section would include all call numbers.

At least one library system, the Maricopa County (AZ) Library District, has abandoned Dewey altogether in one branch. The Perry Branch Library, a joint 28,000-square-foot school media center and public library, opened in 2007, and its entire 31,000-item collection is shelved by topic and alphabetized by author's last name—similar to what is done in bookstores. Based on the success of the "Dewey-less library," the Maricopa County Library District has decided that its next new branch (which opened in November 2008), the 47,000-square-foot Queen Creek Branch Library, would also feature merchandising and be Dewey-less.

According to Harry Courtright, Maricopa's director and county librarian, the reaction among the library's customers to the "Dewey-less library" is quite positive. Staff have to deal with few directional questions because of the visible and high-quality signage. The library is using the Book Industry Study Group subject categories found in bookstores. Although each of the subject areas was originally organized alphabetically by author, after a few months staff members rearranged the materials in alphabetical order by title in response to customer requests!

A similar approach has been adopted by the Frankfort Public Library in Illinois. It has even developed a logo; meet Dewey de Frankfort.[6]

Yet another option along the classification continuum (keep Dewey, no Dewey, or something new) is the creation of a new classification system designed to better meet the needs of a merchandised collection. The staff of the Markham Public Library (ON, Canada) have created the C3 system—the Customer Centred Classification system, which divides the world's knowledge into two broad categories: a personal or inward-looking perspective and a worldly or externally focused perspective. A four-digit number is assigned to each topic—only a four-digit number is found on the spine label of each item, as illustrated in Figure 5.4 (p. 44). (The number is never Cuttered, so the decimal point and the following numbers are not needed, which makes shelving of materials go much quicker.) Items are filed alphabetically by the author's last name within each C3 topic or category.

In addition, new topics are only slowly introduced into the Dewey classification system. As topics grow quickly, for example the personal computer and the Internet, a Dewey area will noticeably "bulge" as Cutter numbers are added and added. A merchandising topical approach provides much more flexibility.

Figure 5.4. Spine Label for the Customer Centered Classification System.
Photo courtesy of the Markham Public Library

Recently the remodeled and expanded Markham Village branch library was opened using the C3 system. According to Catherine Biss, director of the Markham Public Library:

> Customers love the new and expanded Markham Village Library which is merchandized for customer ease of browsing. The Collection is organized according to our internally developed classification system, C3 or "Customer-Centred Classification." This four digit numerical classification system facilitates bookstore style browsability along with the specificity to locate items that Dewey provided. An added benefit is that materials are easier to re-shelve, enabling a quicker turn-around time to the next customer. Staff is currently in the process of further refining C3, but for the customer, it seems to be working just fine without a lot of explanation![7]

RESULTS OF MERCHANDISING

As previously noted, use of the library's collection increases, often dramatically, as a result of introducing merchandising, as reflected in percent increase in annual circulation and circulation per capita. However, the merchandised collection is not the first destination when an individual visits the library. Envirosell, a retail store consulting firm, completed a study on behalf of the San Jose and Hayward (CA) Public Libraries in 2007.[8] The firm tracked 269 patrons as they moved about a branch library, interviewed another 240 patrons as they were leaving the library, and analyzed the movements of people in three libraries using more than 350 hours of videotape. The results of the study found that although the Internet Café was the most popular first destination, the merchandised areas did receive a significant amount of foot traffic during the average 30-minute visit to a library. Self-service and self-navigation are very important to most library customers.

More recently, Envirosell completed a study involving four libraries from the Metropolitan Library System located in Illinois.[9] The research team analyzed more than 750 hours of video footage, and some 267 customers were interviewed as they were leaving the library. More than two-thirds of the people visiting the library did not come to the library with a specific need, and thus there is an opportunity to appeal to their "wants." One-third of circulating materials were audiovisual items, and these items would have more appeal if placed in easily browsable displays (merchandised). A majority of people coming to the library were alone, and they spent less than 10 minutes in the library. Most library signage was "not seen" by library customers because the signage was not attractive and not placed in sightlines. Finally, because customers are primarily interested in browsing materials, collections must be organized for browsing.

What is striking when comparing the results of these two studies is that the library customers' behavior is very different. This emphasizes the need to very clearly understand the needs of the customer and to design the library facility and its services from the

outside-in.

OBSTACLES TO MERCHANDISING

Some librarians suggest that although they are interested in merchandising, they find it difficult to implement because of budget and space constraints. Clearly new display fixtures and furniture and signage will cost money that may be difficult to find in the budget. However, it is possible for a library that embraces merchandising to move in an incremental (or step-by-step) manner rather than doing one big makeover (which would consume a big chunk of the budget). Every library building is constrained by space, so the issue is: What is the best utilization of the space? Despite the obstacles, it is possible, with some creativity and planning, to implement merchandising in your library.

IMPLICATIONS OF MERCHANDISING

If a library is going to embrace merchandising in more than a casual way, implications for several areas must be considered, including the collection, the online catalog, the staffing mix, space and furnishings, and jargon and tradition.

The Collection

Clearly merchandising a library's collection is not a one-solution-fits-all approach to delivering library services. The collection, as characterized by the type of materials, its age, and the choice of titles in both fiction and nonfiction, must be tailored to meet the needs of its service community. This is amply demonstrated by the experiences of the Denver Public Library. Merchandising techniques were implemented at the Schlessman Branch, and items were "flying off the shelves." The same techniques when applied at a different branch didn't work. The reason? Each library was serving a different population with differing needs.

A merchandised collection must be appealing to the customer. Thus, a library should carefully review circulation statistics for each item (easily available with the library's integrated library system) and extensively weed its collection as part of the merchandising effort.

Placing merchandised materials near the circulation area will allow customers to browse and respond to "impulse" selections.

The Online Catalog

Clearly adopting the use of merchandising techniques will not eliminate the need for the library's online catalog. However, it will likely require changing and clarifying the display of location-related information. The item will no longer have a call number, but rather a subject area. One handy method, found in some online catalogs, is to display a map of the library indicating the location of the desired item.

The Staffing Mix

Introducing merchandising in a library is likely to have some major impacts on the number and types of staff. One of the obvious needs is to ensure that staff members periodically visit the display areas so that the displays can be refreshed frequently. Display "holes" must be filled quickly! Some libraries have created a new type of page or clerical position who is always roving in the public areas, refreshing the displays and responding to customer queries about the location of specific items or providing directions to other display areas.

If merchandising a library's collection results in increased usage of the collection, which is the experience of many libraries, then additional clerical staff may be needed to check in items that have been returned to the library and get them back on the shelves in a timely manner. In addition, staff may need to adjust the frequency with which the book return bins are emptied to help ensure the most popular items are available for borrowing. Alternatively, libraries can turn to technology in the form of self-check in/book-sorting equipment to help them cope with increased usage. At the Markham Public Library (ON, Canada), the combination of a heavily merchandised collection and a newly expanded and renovated branch has resulted in a 50 percent increase in circulation. No additional staff were hired following the renovation, which saw the branch grow from 20,000 to 30,000 square feet. The library is able to manage the increased usage through the use of an automated book sorter.

Space and Furnishings

If the library is going to install some merchandising furnishings, it is likely that it will need to rearrange some of the space within the library. Depending on the amount of merchandising, some of the traditional library shelving may have to be removed. The goal is to establish a traffic flow that is logical and encourages the customer to browse the library's collection.

Clearly moving to some form of merchandising means that the library will have to remove a portion of its traditional spine-out shelving to install merchandising furnishings, not to mention doing a thorough weeding of the collection. If merchandising a collection means that it is more intensively used, as evidenced by a higher turnover rate for the collection, then the community is receiving higher value for its investment in the library's collection. If a collection of 100,000 volumes housed in spine-out shelving has a turnover rate of four times a year, then a merchandised collection of 80,000 volumes only needs to achieve a turnover rate of five to achieve the same circulation levels. However, the library has saved a considerable amount of money (20,000 volumes times the purchase price plus processing costs), which could be spent in other ways to improve library service to its community.

Libraries often do not see themselves as business entities. Any well-run business uses ROI (return on investment) data to determine how efficient it is and how well it uses its resources. More libraries should conduct ROI analysis on their services to ensure that they are spending their customers' "funds" efficiently and effectively.

Jargon and Tradition

One of the continuing ironies of the library profession is its insistence on calling a classification number a "call number." *Call number* is a carryover from when libraries had closed stacks and a library customer had to fill out a call slip using a call number. With the exception of the Library of Congress and a few other large research libraries, the vast majority of libraries, certainly public libraries, have not had closed stacks in a long time. One alternative to the call number, adopted by a few libraries, is a "location number." Such a change in terminology helps library customers understand the function of the call number—oops, the location number.

In a similar vein, Michael Casey asked in a recent library blog (www.librarycrunch.com), "Why do we place author-name spine labels on hardcover books when staff and customers can find the same books in a book store without labels? How much do we spend each year to make and place (and replace) those labels—not just the sticker cost but staff time?" Every library might want to consider this question: "Is this a real value-added activity for the library's customers?"

CONCLUSION

A customer-focused library must ask fundamental questions about the total experience of visiting a library and the process of finding materials of interest from the customer's perspective. Is the customer likely to find things of interest if the collection is merchandised? Should the total collection be merchandised, or only some portion of it?

NOTES

1. Ezra Schwartz, "The Iceberg Problem—Is the Investment in Our Collections Visible to Patrons?" *Against the Grain* 16 no. 6 (December 2004–January 2005): 28, 30–32.

2. Nicole Heintzelman, Courtney Moore, and Joyce Ward, "Are Reference Books Becoming an Endangered Species?" *Public Libraries* 47, no. 5 (September/October 2008): 63.

3. The South Jersey Regional Library Cooperative, *Trading Spaces: Reinventing the Library Environment Project* (2004). Available at www.sjrlc.org/tradingspaces/.

4. *Libraries—The San Jose Way* (n.d.). Available at www.sjlibrary.org/about/sjpl/sjway/index.htm.

5. Dave Genesy, "Take the Merchandising Test," *American Libraries* 37, no. 4 (April 2006): 69.

6. For more Free Dewey information, visit deweyfree.com/.

7. Personal communication, November 25, 2008.

8. Envirosell, *San Jose Public Libraries and Hayward Public Libraries: Final Report* (February 16, 2007). Available at www.sjlibrary.org/about/sjpl/sjway/SVPL-HPL_final_report.pdf.

9. Envirosell, *Envirosell Final Report for the Metropolitan Library System* (April 29, 2008). Available at www.mls.lib.il.us/consulting/envirosell.asp.

6

Library Services

The three Rs—reading, 'riting, and 'rithmetic—are no longer enough. We must add the three Cs—computing, critical thinking, and capacity for change.

—Fred Gluck[1]

One of the difficulties facing a library is that in its desire to provide efficient services, the service itself becomes fairly routine or generic. A generic service is not a good way to differentiate the library from its competitors. The challenge is to design a service encounter that is meaningful and a pleasant experience. A service experience can be great if three things are present: visibility, customer engagement, and positive feelings and perceptions.

VISIBILITY

Customers like to see what is happening. Some restaurants have open kitchens that offer a new layer of experience and a new stimulus to the senses. Creating spaces that are more flexible allows the library to configure the space as various types of customers use the facility throughout the day and night.

ENGAGEMENT

Engagement is a sense that the individual has contributed to an outcome. An individual might interact with a staff member and/or another customer. Engagement creates a far stronger connection among people, services, and the brand. It is the point at which the customer relationship shifts from push to pull—customers want the service and don't really need advertising or reminders to use it. Libraries need to figure out ways to engage their customers, whether they physically visit the library or are virtual visitors, in new and compelling ways. Allowing customers the opportunity to rate an item, leave a review, and participate in small groups that encourage a sense of community are just a few ways to harness the energy of community members.

POSITIVE FEELINGS AND PERCEPTIONS

A positive feeling will result when one's engagement with a service reaches a level at which the library service actually makes the life of an individual better. When a product or service attains this level, it really begins to transcend the vast majority of services and their associated brands and experiences. Many things can engage us (e.g., a video game), but they do not necessarily translate into improved productivity or improve the life of the individual in any meaningful way.

Although being more productive does include task-oriented outcomes such as accomplishing something more efficiently or effectively, it can also move into the softer side of productivity. Things that improve our physical health can help us be more productive. Services that help us move forward intellectually make us more productive. Things that strengthen our psychological well-being make us more productive. Things that save us time make us more productive. But how is it possible to distinguish whether something helps individuals attain higher levels of productivity or merely helps them reach a level of engagement? The answer is not surprising: It is the customers themselves who decide what contributes to their productivity.

The threshold at which a customer achieves productivity is highly personal and specific to each individual. Thus, it becomes incumbent upon librarians to really understand how the library adds value for a specific service, by having a very deep understanding of the needs of each customer segment the library serves.

Recognize that every service interaction can be designed and involves a physical dimension, customer actions, employee actions while interacting with a customer, and support processes (that do not directly involve the customer). Support processes include all of those "back room" activities found in libraries, such as the processing of new materials and returning items to shelves after they are returned to the library. Some libraries delay placing new items in the hands of customers who have been waiting while the item is being processed—the delay can be days or weeks. The goal from the customer's perspective is Now!

Customers also have higher levels of satisfaction when they encounter staff in the library who are friendly and helpful. Staff attitude is a matter of choice—you can choose to be happy and cheerful or not. Some restaurants use a shift meeting, typically held 15 minutes before the shift change, to review menu changes and remind staff that they can choose to be positive and friendly. Some libraries have found that shift meetings remind staff members of the choices they can make on a daily basis. Remember that a welcoming face is a friendly face.

Work to make each customer touch point better. Humanize each customer interaction to make it something of value, rather than a commodity. A commodity is interchangeable and replaceable. It is important to use these customer–staff touch point moments to build relationships. However, it is also important to recognize that a touch point might also occur when a customer is seeking an indication, in the form of a sign or other clues, of the location of a collection or service. Thus, touch point failures, sometimes called points of pain, will lead to customer frustration.

Consider alternatives for delivering an existing service. For example, what would happen if you "blew up" the reference service desk? How would you reinvent the service desk? Do you need a service desk if staff are roving and a customer can make an appointment for more in-depth research assistance? Can service desks be combined? Do you need a separate print reference collection? Can roving staff have a headset phone to provide service? Remember to consider each of the alternatives from the customer's perspective!

Staff who are empowered to break the rules to meet the needs of a customer are helping to create an advocate for the library. Rules should be designed to enhance the customer service experience, rather than saying "no." Bureaucratic rules really engender negative feelings and treat customers as if they are numbers rather than people with unique needs. So work on ways to say "Yes"! Give solutions, not excuses. That is, after all, what the customer wants. And it all starts with the first few words. Say things like "Great! I'm sure there's a way," or "No problem! We can do that!"

WAYFINDING

In addition to visibility, customer engagement, and positive feelings and perceptions, one of the things that has a big impact on service delivery in a physical space is whether the individual understands the environment and feels a sense of being "in control."

Wayfinding is all about knowing where you are, recognizing your destination, and finding your way back out. Among the many things that can improve wayfinding are differentiating among the various areas in the library through differing visual character (colors and texture), using landmarks to provide orientation cues, and providing effective signs at decision points to guide individuals to their destination.

Not surprisingly, it turns out that sign legibility is extremely important, because users rely on identification to navigate efficiently. For signs to be visible upon immediate entry into the building, there must be no obstruction in the line of sight. Signs that have a matte or nonglare finish and characters that contrast well with the background are best. In addition, pictorial signs help overcome language barriers. In addition to the traditional commercially prepared signs, a library can also effectively use a dynamic flat panel sign, on which the content can easily be changed. The Carnegie Library in Pittsburgh has a Web-based system that allows staff to quickly and easily prepare computer-printed signs using various templates. This ensures consistent signage throughout the library system.[2]

Several studies have shown that as floor plan complexity increases, wayfinding performance decreases, and textual signage is the most effective in reducing wayfinding errors—wrong turns or backtracking.[3] One quick way of assessing the ease of wayfinding in a building is to count the number of directional questions received at all service desks. If 10 percent or more of the questions being asked are directional, then the library has a wayfinding problem!

Another study found that libraries typically failed to provide clear sight lines to signs, signs were often poorly positioned, and there was a sense of visual clutter (too many signs—and thus the recommendation that *less is more*!).[4] Often the library accumulates signs that are generated by library staff rather than using a professional sign maker. These staff-created signs are typically "one-time" solutions to a problem. One library found that they had more than 200 signs (excluding shelf range indicators), and of these, only 7 percent were professionally made.[5] Have you ever seen a handmade sign at a major bookstore? Not too often.

Some libraries (e.g., the University of Rochester in New York) have given cameras to users and asked them to take pictures of things they find confusing in the library. The results typically astonish library staff members. In some ways this should not be too surprising—library staff members become very familiar with the library and its arrangements, and those things become second nature (thus, no need for wayfinding).

Many libraries suffer from an information overload problem because of excessive clutter. Customers have difficulty discerning the differences among items posted on a bulletin board, directional signs, policy signs, handouts, bus schedules, and so forth.

Interestingly, staff expect users to ask for help, have plenty of time, and understand how the library is organized. Yet the evidence suggests that many people (especially men) will not approach a service desk, do not understand how the library is organized (and thus do not know all about the service offerings), and will only spend short periods of time in a library.[6]

It may be helpful to organize library messages into a consistent framework using four broad categories, as suggested by MAYA Design for the Carnegie Library of Pittsburgh:

- **Orient or direct** displays show the location and relationships of physical spaces and provide directions to major areas. Such displays are located at decision points and are uniquely distinguished so as to capture the customer's attention. In addition to traditional signage, the library might employ a large flat-screen display.

- **Identify** names areas, objects, and activities. This will help customers know they are heading in the right direction or are in the right place.

- **Educate**, explain, instruct, and inform customers as a way of encouraging self-sufficiency. Such signs provide just-in-time contextual messages: "How to . . ." or "Did you know . . . ?"

- **Connect** messages assist in linking activities and resources.

The first impressions of a library and its usability are important. They ultimately affect whether users come back to the library in the long term. The goal for any library is to make wayfinding easier for all users using *large and colorful* signage and visual clues, such as color and design of carpeting and the color of the walls, to the location and organization of various components in the library building.

THE NEW CUSTOMER

The reactions of individuals who come to the library for the first time can be quite disconcerting. They will likely complete a library card application form (paper-based or using a computer workstation) and receive a library card. And that's it! Over the course of a three- to four-year period, as many as half of the people who come to the library and receive a library card never return to the library!

And yet, with just a brief investment of time, each of these individuals could be personally welcomed to "his or her" library and given a short, two- to three-minute orientation to the layout of the library and where various collections and services are located. This orientation would help the new library customer become familiar with the library and make the individual more comfortable with the surroundings in the library. These customers are more likely to return to the library again and again.

Yet the reality is that libraries do very little to retain the customers who have found them! Does the library director send a personal note of welcome? Is there any follow-up with new customers or customers who have not used the library for some period of time? Why not?

THE WORDS WE USE

Over time, the library profession builds up and uses its own vocabulary or jargon. When reinventing the library from the customer's perspective, it is time to challenge the use of jargon and begin to describe collections and services with terms that customers would use and understand.

Rather than *reference*, perhaps we should use *research* (which describes the broad concept of reference) and use *research* in signage (the Research Desk rather than the Reference Desk). Other libraries have used "Information Desk" rather than Reference Desk. The Carnegie Library of Pittsburgh uses a sign above a service desk that says, "Ask a Librarian" rather than Reference and "Customer Service" rather than Circulation. Librarians use the word *periodicals* (and even worse, *serials*) rather than *magazines*. There are more examples of jargon that a library customer will encounter, which need to be identified and then excised from use, such as "claims returned," "claims never had," "Boolean searching," "citation," "monograph," and so forth.

The language staff members use when talking with a customer is even more important. Provide staff with examples of language that it is best to use or not to use in situations that they encounter repeatedly. For example, "Our records show a balance of . . ." is better than "You owe . . . ," or "Let's see how we can make this work for you," rather than "It's our policy [to say no]."

DRESS CODE

It always surprises me how resistant librarians are to the concept of a dress code for staff. One frustrating aspect of getting a question answered in a library is figuring out who is a staff member (because staff typically do not wear a uniform shirt or visible name badge). As a result, a library visitor is likely to drift away and not return when he or she is unsure where to turn for help or whom to ask. This is especially true of someone who is new to the library and is having difficulty cracking the library jargon and understanding the organization of the library.

Ask most library staff members if they are committed to good customer service, and the answer is a unanimous "yes." Yet this same group of employees consistently ignores the fact that wearing a uniform shirt would do much to improve customer service in a library.

HOURS

The hours that a library is open will have a dramatic impact on how much it is used. It is also important to recognize that in many households both adults are working, so they are unable to visit a library until after 6 P.M. during the week. Historically, libraries have been open Monday through Friday during normal business hours. This is convenient for staff members, but it is not convenient for library customers. A much better place to start is to examine when the library is open from the perspective of the customer. Thus, a library should start with Sunday hours, add Saturday hours, and then figure out the hours during the week when the library is the busiest and schedule accordingly.

CONCLUSION

The time for action is NOW! Libraries are being out-competed by retail establishments. Library offerings are perceived as less varied, flexible, and sophisticated that those presented by bookstores, cafes, and bars. Bookstores are redesigning their stores to offer customers the ability to download music, create custom professional-bound books, research the family tree, and learn to use digital toys. Libraries rarely offer comfortable seating in proximity to a coffee and food cafe, background music, or even alcoholic beverages. Digitization and the Internet are going to have an enormous impact on library services, and the perception of the library is likely to become even more marginalized.

One of the historic strengths of the library has been its ability to assemble a high-quality collection and thus be a trusted source of information in a community. Yet this wonderful resource is increasingly being ignored by people who want to access sources that are immediately and widely accessible for use and reuse.

Libraries must learn to put customers first. Libraries must immerse themselves in the Web 2.0 revolution so that the library is a part of the conversation about books, videos, music, and other things that interest the community, rather than sitting on the sidelines being ignored.

The challenge is to develop an **outside-in** *discipline* that requires the library to have an explicit customer-based reason for everything it does.

The focus is not so much about serving customers, it's

listening to customers,

asking customers for information,

being prepared to serve customers on their terms,

gaining a better understanding of customers and their various needs,

surprising and delighting customers,

being memorable,

anticipating and being responsive,

striving to get customers to return time and again,

getting customers so excited that they rave about the library to their friends,

building the library brand so that it is more than books, and

creating a library experience from the

outside-in!

NOTES

1. Quoted in Tom Peters, *The Pursuit of WOW!: Every Person's Guide to Topsy-Turvy Times* (New York: Vintage Books, 1994), 259.

2. Beth Dempsey, "Designing Buildings and Services from the End User's Viewpoint Transforms Access for Everyone," *Library Journal* 130, no. 20 (December 15, 200): 72–75.

3. See, for example, Michael J. O'Neill, "Effects of Signage and Floor Plan Configuration on Wayfinding Accuracy," *Environment & Behavior* 23, no. 5 (September 1991): 553–74.

4. Gale Eaton, Machael Vocino, and Melanie Taylor, "Evaluating Signs in a University Library," *Collection Management* 16, no. 3 (1992): 81–101.

5. Ellen Bosman and Carol Rusinek, "Creating the User-Friendly Library by Evaluating Patron Perceptions of Signage," *Reference Services Review* (Spring 1997): 71–82.

6. Envirosell, *Best Practices for the Customer-Focused Library* (Burr Ridge, IL: Metropolitan Library System, 2008). Available at www.mls.lib.il.us/consulting/envirosell.asp. See also Paco Underhill, *Why We Buy: The Science of Shopping* (London: Texere, 2000).

7

Information Technology

Do not start with what you have now. Rather, create the picture of the future. Otherwise you will be constrained by growing what you have rather than creating what you need.

—Alan Weiss[1]

Libraries are consistently slow to adopt and adapt to the use of information technology (IT). Libraries and librarians are not demanding the best from their vendors or their staff. Libraries spend too much time trying to get IT to work rather than putting IT to work to advance the service delivery capabilities of the library. The pace of change on the Web is quite rapid, whereas the pace of change in library IT environments is quite slow. Thus the gap between the two environments simply gets bigger each year.

It is safe to say that in general, library online catalogs and Web sites suck! There are a few exceptions, but almost universally, library Web sites are inward looking and provide little reason for people to return again and again. Often the content of the library's Web site is fairly old, and it is difficult to navigate to find content of value. If people had to attend a bibliographic instruction class to use Amazon, then Amazon would not stay in business for long.

It is true that some libraries have completed usability studies to improve their Web sites or online catalogs, but in general these libraries are few in number, and the improvements have only marginal results from the customer's perspective.

THE NEW LIBRARY CATALOG

Research demonstrates that only a small proportion of library customers use the library's online catalog, and because the catalog does not return "Google-like results," people are often confused. The reality is that the information landscape is crowded—Google, Amazon, Yahoo, eBay, ESPN, and so forth—and the library is not even a blip on people's radar screens, as evidenced by the OCLC *Perceptions* report.[2]

It is really surprising how many libraries still consider that they are in the information business. Almost every library is located on a cul-de-sac, far from the on-ramp to the "Information Superhighway." The user of a library online catalog or OPAC often has no clear starting point, as well as having trouble identifying an appropriate electronic resource, which may or may not be searchable using the library's OPAC.

Some have suggested that libraries should abandon traditional subject headings and rely solely on user-generated tags to describe items in the library's collection. However, the solution does not need to be taxonomy versus folksonomy—it can be both!

One interesting online catalog is the AquaBrowser. Its search results are presented in two related areas on the screen. On the left-hand side is a faceted search display that shows the word or phrase that is related to the search request. This assists the user in exploring alternatives word or phrases and to see what is retrieved. The right-hand portion of the screen presents the bibliographic record and a copy of the book jacket, if available.

Recently, several libraries have been experimenting with a concept called the "social OPAC." A social OPAC provides users with a set of tools that allows them (and encourages them) to rate, review, comment, and tag items in the library catalog. The whole idea of a social OPAC is to unleash the power of the "we" through the active participation of those who use the catalog. It is possible to unleash the power of crowds in your library.[3]

A social OPAC removes the shackles of bibliographic control, long established and cherished by the library profession, by encouraging people who are interested in books, movies, music, and so forth to find a place where they can share with one another. The online catalog provides results in ways that are similar to those provided by Google, which are based on popularity. Among the things that a social OPAC provides are (1) the ability to save links to an item in another product (wherever that product may be), (2) the ability to use an online catalog tool in other services such as Facebook, (3) the ability for users to create and publish lists of their favorite books (and for the user—not the library—to establish the privacy level for this list), and (4) access to other Web 2.0 technologies.

Implementing a social OPAC, sometimes called a SOPAC, is going to be difficult for a library because the library is no longer in control. If people are going to participate, they need to know that what they do will be accepted. Certainly safeguards are needed to guard against abuse, but other social network sites have developed and published "rules of conduct" for a site that are much more responsive in identifying and correcting problems when they crop up. Clearly librarians are still trying to get their heads around the concept of social networking and have yet to recognize that social media are all about diverse, community-generated content. The lesson other organizations have learned about social networking is that they must "let go of control" so that the community becomes excited about the possibilities of being involved with the library.

Perhaps the most visible of the social OPAC proponents is John Blyberg at the Darien Library in Connecticut (see the library Web site at www.darienlibrary.org/). The software John has developed is made available as open source (visit www.thesocialopac.net) and is called SOPAC 2.0. This social catalog features faceted browsing and tag clouds and allows patrons to add reviews, comments, and ratings. The hope is that as other libraries implement SOPAC 2.0, the base of reviews, ratings, and comments will grow substantially.

Search here.
darienlibrary.org
September 1, 2008

BiblioCommons is a social discovery system that allows faceted searching (a faceted classification system allows the assignment of multiple classifications to an object, enabling the classifications to be ordered in multiple ways, rather than in a single, predetermined, taxonomic order) and easier user commenting and tagging, which replaces a library's traditional online catalog. The traditional online catalog is all about finding. Users can earn credits for adding "a comment, tag, summary, similar title, recommendations, age suitability, content notice or quotation" or creating a list. Those credits can be used for chances at prizes or other rewards determined by the library, to pay fines or fees. The system includes "share with a friend" links and a shelf browser with cover images. BiblioCommons can be used with any of the commercial integrated library systems (ILS) in the marketplace. Libraries are able to share commentary with other libraries.

Primo, offered by ExLibris, provides a single interface to search different systems. The system includes a "did you mean" feature as well as faceted navigation. Libraries can share tags, ratings, and reviews. Encore, Innovative Interface's next generation discovery tool, displays both subject headings and community-contributed tags. Summon, developed by Serials Solution, has a Google-like single search that moves the user into the discovery phase very quickly. The Library Corp.'s LS2 has a good visual design.

The following libraries are experimenting with the concept of a social OPAC:

- The Hennepin County Library.

- The Ann Arbor (MI) District Library Virtual Card Catalog in which users can create on-the-fly vintage-looking catalog cards and even add notes in the margin. These cards can be saved in a personal file and/or be e-mailed to someone. Users can decide to make their card catalogs publicly available.

- The University of Pennsylvania Libraries' ongoing project in social tagging in their catalog, called PennTags, which allows an individual to add phrases and comments to a bibliographic record.

- The Clinton Macomb (MI) Public Library, which allows users to save lists.

- The Hong Kong University Science & Technology Library's SmartCAT.

- The Plymouth State University (New Hampshire), which has developed Scriblio, an open-source content management system and online catalog with faceted searching.

- Villanova University's VUFind, which is an open source resource layer that replaces a library's ILS-based OPAC.

One of the obvious implications of a library wanting to experiment with its own social OPAC is that it will require hiring talented computer programmers. And finding talented programmers who are knowledgeable about a library is even more difficult. We can only hope that the ILS vendors will recognize the need to develop a new generation online catalog that is much more responsive to the needs of library customers. In addition, libraries should be demanding that vendors provide application programming interface (API) tools and deliver search results using standard protocols, so a library can mix and match products to best meet its needs.

In addition, to make the social OPAC a reality the library will also have to purchase additional disk space, a server or two, and some software. The definition of the social OPAC will likely evolve and morph over time, so the concept will embrace more and more.

To learn more about your customers' experience in using your library's existing online catalog, ask if you can sit and observe people as they use the catalog. Ask them to verbalize what they like and don't like about it. Ask what they would like to see in the way of improvements. Who should be involved in this process? Why, the library director and the senior management team, of course, so they can truly appreciate the library's catalog and the challenges it presents from the customer's perspective!

THE LIBRARY WEB SITE

The Internet is the ultimate customer-empowering experience—one click and you are out of there! One click! If the Web site is difficult to use—click! If the user gets lost while using a Web site—click! If the text on a Web site is difficult to read—click! If the Web site makes finding things of value difficult—click! If a library's Web site requires the user to go on a scavenger hunt—click! The reality is that people don't have the time or patience to figure things out. A library Web site should not provoke the user into exclaiming

Don't make me THINK![4]

As people use a variety of Web sites such as Amazon, Google, Southwest Airlines, YouTube, Flickr, and so forth, they develop a mental model of what a Web site should look and feel like. When your library Web site does not behave in similar ways, users gets frustrated and—click! Remember that the individual who controls the mouse—click!—has the power.

Examining a library's Web site will reveal a great deal about a library. Based on the Web site, is the library progressive, or does it have a very staid perspective? Is the design clean and well organized, or is it cluttered and messy? Is it possible for library customers to become involved with one another (and interested library staff members) using Web 2.0 technology, or is there a restrictive policy? How long has it been since the Web site has been updated or redesigned? What is the message that the library is broadcasting when someone comes to visit?

A majority of library Web sites are designed by librarians who do not have a lot of experience with Web design. The result is often a Web site that, despite the best of intentions, librarians are really comfortable with—and the user is not. The amount of library jargon on library Web sites is simply amazing. And how frequently is the Web site updated to ensure the content is fresh?

Does the signage in a library match that found in the Web site? For a great example of such an approach, check out the Carnegie Library of Pittsburgh Web site—www.carnegielibrary.org. "Ask a Librarian" is featured prominently on the Web site and at the reference desk, oops, the Ask a Librarian service desk.

Library Web sites often provide access to a number of electronic resources (databases), which require the user to learn to use different user interfaces to gain access to these resources.

Not surprisingly, only the most dedicated will persist. Some libraries have tried to use a federated search service, which does provide a single search interface, but the users are frustrated by the inability of the service to de-duplicate search results and present the results in a meaningful way.

There are any number of print and online resources available that provide guidance about improving the usability of Web sites. A large number of techniques can be used to assist in the process of improving usability. Many of these techniques provide the opportunity to involve library customers in the process of improvement. The involvement of customers in improving a library service is not only to be encouraged, but should be a requirement. This way, the library Web site will be improved from the

outside-in!

However, the first questions to ask when assessing the library Web site are who uses it, and for what purposes? Almost all libraries view their Web sites as the place to provide access to content 24/7. Yet even a cursory examination of the Web statistics makes clear that content simply does not have much appeal. The library should focus its Web site on the services it can provide—in-person or remotely—that appeal to the user. The library has to start building connections with people in the community, one user at a time.

Most likely, the typical online library user is not going to be part of the same group of people who actually physically visit the library. The library should create a series of profiles (multiple profiles will be necessary, because different groups of people will be visit the library Web site for different reasons). Once the Web designer has a clear picture of the different types of user as captured in the profile, they then can design a better customer experience.

Library directors, managers, board members, and other staff members should learn about using the library Web site from the customer's perspective. Give your library Web site a test drive and see how easy it is—or isn't—to navigate around the site and perform various tasks. However, don't sit in your office to conduct this test. Sit where your customer sits in your library to get the full experience. Are the keyboards and computer workstations screens clean? Do some keys on the keyboard stick? How long are the response times? Is it easy to print or save materials using a flash drive (computer stick)? Hopefully the experience will be eye-opening even if it may not be pleasant.

Many public libraries, as departments within a city or county, must use the standard Web page template that all the other departments do, which is mandated by the organization's IT department (this makes it easier for the IT department to maintain the Web sites). This does not translate into a positive experience for the library customer. The library director must make the case that the library is different than every other department, and that the library's Web site must have a different look and feel—while still maintaining a link to the city or county Web site.

The main goal for any library Web site is *stickiness*—providing visitors with many reasons to return again and again. This means that the Web site must have more than content and provide tools that are engaging and entertaining and provide ways for social interaction. Many observers have suggested that the primary way to do this is to integrate Web 2.0 tools in the Web site. This is a "technology tools are the answer" approach, which must be resisted until the library has answered a more fundamental questions: What is going to engage the visitor and provide such a compelling experience that the visitor will want to return frequently to the library's Web site? What can be done online that can't be done in the physical library?

There is nothing worse than a blog on a library Web site in which some librarian has posted a few terse comments and photos every two to four weeks because it is expected! The goal is to use the appropriate tools in a way that helps build a bridge between the library and the community. Remember that there are at least five stages that people must go through before they become online library advocates: awareness, participation, engagement, conversation, and affinity (or loyalty).

So what can a library do? Why not invite a group of interested individuals, such as teens or members of a book club, to assume responsibility for a blog that is focused on a very specific topic or interest? Then library staff members can chime in and contribute their "bits" when they are so inclined—hopefully the "bits" will be interesting and reflect a real human being (not an institution). The end result is a conversation rather than a boring mirror that is looking inward toward the library—Hey! Look at us! We are doing neat stuff! Don't ya think? Huh? Anyone there? Hello?

If the library has started to experiment with other social networking tools, such as MySpace, Facebook, Twitter, and LinkedIn, make sure the library "friends" individuals in the local community rather than in other libraries. Get out of the library and go where people hang out, such as the local coffee shop. Start a conversation and hand out business cards. Use online tools to identify people in your community you can connect to. The goal is to help the library build a presence in the online local community, rather than building links to other libraries. It's all a part of answering that question: How will this tool allow the library to create a relationship with a segment of the community that the community values? The library can use other methods to build and maintain relationships with other libraries and librarians using tools available on professional association Web sites.

Recently, National Public Radio went "live" with major changes in its Web site to promote involvement in the community. The goal is to provide a set of tools to facilitate collaboration among NPR's listeners. The library should be focused on answering three questions about the online experience:

- **Function**—What do people want to do? Many people want to search for answers and tell stories. It's not so much the interaction between a librarian and a customer, but providing a platform that encourages and facilitates communication among and between customers, that builds a sense of community. Many libraries have a tradition of recording oral histories of those who live in their community. Why not extend this tradition by providing a set of tools that allows people to share and collaborate?

- **Content**—What do people want to know? The library Web site should present information on the basis of the visitor's prior navigation patterns.

- **Brand**—What will people remember? Promote the benefits of frequent visits. The library brand must resonate with its community and build connections with individuals and groups. For example, the Vancouver (BC, Canada) Public Library Web site features photos of its customers as a way to demonstrate a connection with its community.

Scholastic Books has created a new series called <u>The 39 Clues</u>, which ties together a 10-book mystery series with an online gaming environment. The hope of Scholastic is that people will visit the Web site between the release of the next new book every few months, to sustain the interest of the reader. This provides the reader with an incentive to return to the Web site again and again.

In an effort to help integrate the library's Web site into people's lives, the Singapore Public Library encourages people to submit photos (similar to Flickr), which can then be viewed and shared with others. Web 2.0 technologies offer a library many opportunities to add a function or feature to a Web site, but before doing so the library must ask a very important question: Will the library customer find value in this tool or feature? Remember that the reason for using any of the Web 2.0 tools should be in providing a tool that will help the library *engage* its community.

Every library should ask itself the fundamental questions: What is the value proposition for any individual to visit the library's Web site? Why would people want to return again and again? What is the return (value) for the time spent on a library's Web site?

DIGITAL CONTENT

An increasing amount of materials is being digitized—both by libraries and commercial firms. Finding tools for these materials will have to be significantly improved. A library will have to provide a simple means of gaining access to this increasingly large and diverse digital content for its customers. Should the library provide a link to Google Books on its Web site, or build an interface that will search the library catalog and Google Books content simultaneously?

By the way, providing a shopping list of places where digital content is available (the Library of Congress, the British Library, the Smithsonian, Google Books, etc.) is simply not going to work. Such an approach presumes that the user will know what content is to be found at a specific location.

So the challenges relating to digital content for the profession and for each library are considerable and will require much thought, energy, experimentation, and passion.

IT ARCHITECTURE

For the most part, libraries are too constrained by tightly coupled integrated library systems and other systems needed to deliver services. Libraries need to be moving to a new IT "environment" that is more open and allows a library to mix and match products and systems. In such an environment the library will be able to preserve its investment in one system while replacing another component with something that will better meet its needs.

It is helpful to think of the library IT environment as being composed of two primary components, sometimes called the front end and the back end. The front end is what library customers and staff members interact with; the back end is where the data are typically stored and manipulated. Note that the back end system can be physically located in a library facility or located in another city or another state. With a loosely coupled systems environment, the library would be able to easily replace an existing module, for example, the online catalog, with another product.

As libraries continue to become even more dependent on technology, information and communication technologies dominate discussions about the future of the library. When considering these issues, it is very important to look at them from the customer's perspective—from the

outside-in!

NOTES

1. Alan Weiss, blog posting at www.ContrarianConsulting.com.

2. Cathy De Rosa, Joanne Cantrell, Diane Cellentani, Janet Hawk, Lillie Jenkins, and Alane Wilson, *Perceptions of Libraries and Information Resources* (Dublin, OH: OCLC, 2005).

3. Barry Liebert and Jon Spector, *We Are Smarter Than Me* (Upper Saddle River, NJ: Wharton School Publishing, 2008).

4. For a wonderful book about usability, see Steve Krug, *Don't Make Me Think!: A Commonsense Approach to Web Usability* (Indianapolis, IN: New Riders, 2006).

8

Library Staffing

The most important thing in your library goes home every night
—your staff.

It seems so obvious: The future of your library is directly tied to the quality of talent you attract and retain. Like most organizations today, the library faces real competition from mega-bookstores and online options such as Amazon. People are much more informed because they have access to a wealth of information via the Internet (some characterize this as trying to drink from a fire hose) on which to base decisions. So the assumption that many libraries have historically made that they are the only game in town is simply no longer valid—if it ever was.

The only sustainable competitive advantages for many organizations, including (in my view) the public library, are innovation and superior customer service—both of which come from extremely talented people. So identifying, recruiting, and retaining talented people is a basic requirement for the success of any library.

Although attracting top talent is very important, it is equally important to find talent that works and plays well with other equally talented individuals. All these individuals have to be held accountable for being able to collaborate, share knowledge, and work as a part of an effective team.

As Jim Collins noted in *Good to Great*, it's equally as important to get the right people on the bus as it is to get the wrong people off.[1] Once the right people are in place, they can be involved in helping choose the library's vision and strategies.

RECRUITING STAFF

Customer-facing staff members must really like interacting with and helping customers. Many public service staff members in a large number of libraries do not seem to find much joy in their jobs. As libraries change the way they deliver services and reinvent the library so that it is more appealing to members of their community, a "people person" becomes an even more important asset. Look for creative and adaptive people, as they are likely to bring a unique perspective to a problem. A person who is passionate and has the right "attitude" is much more important than someone with really good job skills that will meet a short-term need. In short, hire for attitude and flexibility, and train for service.

An in-depth and thoughtful hiring process is crucial to the library's success. Interview questions must be probing and ask candidates to provide illustrations of how they interact with people in a variety of circumstances. Get a number of staff members involved in the interview process. For the really adventurous, the library could involve some customers in the selection process. Southwest Airlines invites its frequent flyers to participate in interviewing and "auditioning" potential flight attendants. From the customer's perspective, the possibility of helping to select flight attendants is quite appealing. The airline must maintain a waiting list of customers who would like to participate!

Once someone has been hired, make sure that the new employee is assigned an appropriate mentor to smooth the transition into the new job. Specific job skills are important, but much more important is helping the new staff member understand and contribute to the organizational culture of the library.

With each new staff member, the library has an opportunity of seeing itself with fresh eyes. Ask each of these new staff members the following questions:

- When you walked into the library, what was your impression?
- What could be done to improve the aesthetics of the interior of the building?
- Do you have any suggestions for improving the exterior of the building?
- What are we doing that surprised you?
- What should we be doing that we are not?
- What are your impressions of the signage in this building?
- How would you rate our staff on friendliness?
- Have you visited our Web site? What are your impressions?

This advice about hiring the right people is certainly not unique—lots of people have been saying this for some time. For example, as mentioned previously, Jim Collins discusses the importance of getting the right people on the bus. However, what most organizations (including libraries) don't do is develop a set of procedures to ensure that *only* the right people are hired. It is necessary to go beyond the typical process of advertising, reviewing resumes, interviewing a few candidates, and making a selection. Involve many of your staff members in the interview process. Have candidates interact with staff members. And most important, don't "settle" for second best!

DEVELOPING STAFF

The value of training can be demonstrated by the fact that the Walt Disney Company spends more time and energy on training its "trash picker-uppers" than on any other group of employees. This is done because visitors asking for directions and a myriad of other questions approach these theme park employees most frequently. The trash sweepers probably spend more time answering questions than they do sweeping. Disney has learned that knowing the answers is as important as knowing how to provide directions and respond to questions. So they provide training about the "what" as well as the "how."

Providing training opportunities for library staff members is important so that individuals can enhance their job skills and prepare for promotion opportunities that may arise. Staff in bookstores are routinely cross-trained (including how to make lattes), but cross-training in libraries is generally the exception rather than the rule. Although training can be done in-house, there are other sources for training, including online opportunities offered through professional associations, community colleges, and professional training organizations.

Zappos, the online shoe company, is noteworthy for the investment it makes in training new employees. They go through a five-week customer loyalty boot camp. When it's over, they're offered $2,000 to quit. Approximately 2 to 3 percent of new hires accept this offer. (The company wishes more new hires would take them up on the offer! (Those new hires who opt for the money and leave realize after their training that they are not a good fit for the culture and work ethic of Zappos.) Zappos defined a set of core values that helps keep them focused on the right things:

- Deliver "WOW" through service.
- Embrace and drive change.
- Create fun and a little weirdness.
- Be adventurous, creative, and open-minded.
- Pursue growth and learning.
- Build open and honest relationships with communication.
- Build a positive team and family spirit.
- Do more with less.
- Be passionate and determined.
- Be humble.

What is interesting about these values is that the focus is on the customer and the employee —not the company. Consider your library. Have you articulated a set of values? Many libraries have. Now consider the perspective of these values. I bet the focus is primarily on the library and only indirectly on the customer!

It is important for a library to realize that it needs to go beyond providing training opportunities. A whole suite of activities, including coaching, mentoring, and self-directed learning must be addressed. Those who will be providing the training must start with the end in mind. Trainers and instructors have to be able to see the big picture to assemble the necessary pieces of instruction. Library staff members must be continuously encouraged to grow and learn.

Most of the training that is provided typically does not look too deeply into the value or success of the training session other than "did we do good?" Donald Kirkpatrick has suggested that there are four levels of evaluation of training programs:

Level 1—Traditional one-page evaluation form: "Did you like the training?"

Level 2—Determining what the student learned.

Level 3—The degree to which the learned skills are applied on the job.

Level 4—Tying training to the bottom line.[2]

Using an evaluation approach such as Level 3 will help a library make sure that it receives value for its training expenditures.

Just because you have a degree doesn't mean that you stop learning!

ENERGIZING STAFF

If a library is going to reinvent itself to become more relevant to the lives of its customers, that organization is considering embracing a great deal of change. Yet the staff of many libraries—professional or clerical level staff—are still very resistant to change. Often the organizational culture of the library is firmly committed to "resistance to change" as the standard operating procedure.

To overcome resistance to change, the library director has to paint pictures in conversations of what a customer-focused library will look and act like. These pictures should be designed to energize the staff so that they become more welcoming of change. When everyone understands the direction that the library is headed and how each individual's job contributes to the overall goals, the library will become a truly energized organization.

The majority of library staff members are hidden behind walls from the library's customers. Ask staff to spend more time interacting with customers and less time behind a service desk or in their offices. Roving staff, assuming they are recognizable as staff, will find they spend more face-to-face time with customers if they are up and away from a service desk. "Blow up" your service desks—they are too large and are a barrier to providing high-quality service. Consider eliminating or consolidating service desks to free up space for more valuable assets: computer workstations, merchandising displays, and so forth. Insist that librarians spend more time outside the library interacting with their existing and potential customers in other community settings.

Some libraries use mystery shoppers as a way to track the levels of customer service, examine the cleanliness of facilities, and identify wayfinding problems.

Asking people to answer essential questions will get staff members to really focus on what is important. Among the essential questions for a customer-focused library are the following:

- How does the library add value for each market segment?

- How does each staff member add value for the library customers?

- How do we need to work differently to accomplish our goals?

- What data are we gathering from our customers that will help us better understand their lives and needs?

- What do our customers care about most? Ask various customer segments to define their "care abouts." Ask each customer segment to prioritize its "care abouts."

- How much time do librarians spend in the community learning about the needs of their customers?

- What opportunities does the library have to truly delight our customers?

- In what ways do we operate now that makes us "difficult to do business with?"

- What performance measures will help us track our progress in reaching our goals?

The OCLC report *From Awareness to Funding* found that "passionate librarians who are involved in the community make a real difference."[3] In particular, five attributes can be used to define a "passionate" librarian: an advocate for lifelong learning, fervent about making the library relevant again, knowledgeable about the community, aware of all that the library offers, and well-educated. A *passionate librarian* will reinforce the perception that the library can be a transformational force in people's lives.

From the perspective of the community and the customer, the majority of librarians are largely invisible to the community they serve. Rarely does a librarian ventured out beyond the bounds of the building and interact with the community to better understand its needs.

RECOGNIZING STAFF

Most public libraries have constraints on the ways in which a staff member can be rewarded. However, library managers can do a variety of things to recognize individual staff members, which staff will enjoy. Among these activities are the following:

- *Find their strengths.* Recognize significant accomplishments and heroic acts and go above and beyond the call of duty, which too often go unnoticed, unrecognized, and uncelebrated. Then share these stories with other staff members.

- *Publicize your staff exploits.* Share these stories of staff accomplishments with customers, stakeholders, and other staff members.

- *Say thank-you more often.* Use conversations, e-mail, voice mail, or whatever means you have to say thanks again and again. Be specific about mentioning what the individual did.

- *Encourage others to share staff activities that delight customers.*

- *Send handwritten thank-you notes.* Notes will make your staff members' day! They tell people that you care enough to take the time to write a personal note.

- *Provide candy, pastries, flowers, or ice cream.* In short, celebrate, celebrate!

- *Spend more time walking around the library.* Chat with staff members and with customers. Personally discover those WOW moments and share them with others.

RESISTANCE TO CHANGE

One of the biggest challenges facing a library that wants to become a customer-focused library is resistance to change among some staff members. This resistance to change is often manifested by the fact that the library has, over time, created a culture that does not reward risk taking, and departments within the library are more like silos with very strong walls. The sad fact is that mature organizations, such as libraries, will have a much more difficult time taking risks, experimenting, and creating innovation.

Too often a library will engage in a detailed form of planning a new service. Libraries can go through so much *analysis* to develop the perfect service that it results in *paralysis!*[4] Rather, try things. Be fast and learn fast! Ask your customers for feedback as you roll out a "prototype." Experiment and tinker.

The good news is that embracing change, creating a culture that rewards risk, and building teamwork are things that a library can improve. The key, not surprisingly, is to create a disciplined approach to the process of monitoring projects and change. This process must be disciplined and repeatable for identifying, clarifying, prioritizing, assigning responsibility, setting targets, tracking the progress of implementation, and rewarding success. In short, what gets measured (and rewarded) gets done.

> *It is not the strongest of the species that survive, nor the most intelligent, but the ones most responsive to change.*
> —Charles Darwin

William Bridges has noted that the management of change is really about two things: managing events and managing emotions about those events. It is as important to describe for library staff what is *not changing* as it is to describe what *is changing*.[5]

Collaboration is essential; experimentation should be a regular visitor. Innovative leaders are comfortable with uncertainty, have open minds, and are receptive to ideas from different disciplines. Although collaboration opens up doors of opportunity, it is also crucial for the library to know the direction it is moving and to say no when an interesting, but distracting, opportunity presents itself. The hardest thing for many librarians to say is "No thanks."

Certainly any library should involve the library staff when it is exploring the future. Listen to what they have to say! However, most important, involve your customers—again and again and in many different ways. Listen to what different market segments have to say! Its one thing to amass a pile of statistics and information about market segments; it is quite another to leave the library and immerse yourself in the daily lives of your customers so that you better understand what they do and why they do it. Remember that people often say one thing and do something quite different.

> Without change, something sleeps inside us, and seldom awakens. The sleeper must awaken.
>
> —Frank Herbert[6]

UNIFORMS

One of the challenges that a customer with a question faces in a library is how to differentiate a staff member from the other people in the library. This difficulty arises because staff in most libraries do not wear a uniform shirt. If an employee badge is worn, often it is clipped at the waist or is on a long lanyard and not clearly visible.

Many libraries do have a dress code, but the code is often stated in terms of what cannot be worn—no jeans, no torn clothing, no T-shirts—you get the idea. If we are concerned about the customer's ability to identify a staff member when needed, doesn't a uniform shirt make sense? Or a vest or a jacket?

CUSTOMER SERVICE

Many libraries provide a little form at service desks that asks for comments from the library's customers—"We want your feedback!" Rather than "what do your think," it might be more revealing and interesting to ask customers "what do you want?" Even better would be to ask, "We want your ideas to make this library better" or "We want your ideas to make this the best possible library."

Clearly the quality of library staff members and the level of service they deliver to your customers, physically and virtually, can help differentiate your library from your competitors. In general, customers have the following expectations:

Reliability   The ability to provide what was promised, on time, dependably and accurately. In other words, customers want you to do what you say you are going to do *when* you say you are going to do it.

Assurance	The knowledge and courtesy of library staff members and their ability to convey trust and confidence.
Empathy	The degree of caring and attention provided to customers so that they are treated as individuals.
Responsiveness	The willingness of staff to assist customers and provide prompt and helpful service. Customers prefer that staff members be proactive rather than having to ask for assistance.
Tangibles	The appearance of physical facilities, equipment, and library staff members.

The only way to build and sustain a culture that embraces consistently superior customer service is to create a process that ensures superb customer service. To get stellar results, it is necessary to define in specific terms and actions exactly what great service looks like and, most important, how to make sure the customer is delighted with every customer interaction.

Given the focus of this book, it is best to create the customer service processes from the perspective of the customer—from the **outside-in!** Once the library has a clear understanding of what each customer segment needs, it can design a set of services that will be most appealing from the customer's perspective.

A business consulting firm asked 362 companies if they thought they delivered superior customer experiences. Interestingly, 95 percent of those surveyed said they were customer focused, and 80 percent said they did deliver a superior experience. Yet when the researchers then asked the customers of these companies about their experiences, only *8 percent* felt that the organization did, in fact, deliver a *superior* customer experience![7]

It will be necessary to develop a set of clear, measurable, and observable customer service behaviors and interactions. These behaviors must be quantifiable and objective and are most powerful when they are developed by library staff who have a thorough understanding of the needs of the customers. Specifically, the library should do the following:

- *Build a set of systems, processes, protocols, and procedures that will ensure the consistent delivery of superior service* (as defined by the customer). Rather than hoping for good service, it is better to design the service so that it is a trainable, repeatable, and observable standard of service excellence.

- *Ensure ongoing training for all service delivery staff members.* Give your staff the tools, skills, and equipment necessary to be successful in meeting and exceeding the service delivery standards. Remember that the goal is to provide customers with an experience that results in their being "delighted" when they leave the library.

- *Consistently track, measure, and analyze the customer service delivery system.* Ask staff to rate their peers. Ask customers to rate their experiences—continuously. Use mystery shoppers. Analyze the complaints you receive. Set high goals and communicate the results of the customer service evaluations.

- *Create a system of lavish praise, celebration, and reward* for those individuals who consistently meet or exceed the service delivery standards.

- *Review the system periodically.* Solicit feedback from customers regularly, based on quantifiable survey results and qualitative responses in the form of focus groups and an analysis of complaints (and compliments). Make any necessary adjustments and provide even more training.

Many libraries use satisfaction surveys to learn how happy their customers are with their products and services. Typically these surveys yield very positive results. However, as many different segments of the economy have discovered, what matters is not what customers say about their level of satisfaction, but whether the value they feel they have received will keep them coming back.

Frederick F. Reichheld found that it was possible to divide the respondents to a customer satisfaction survey into three groups:

Promoters are loyal enthusiasts who give ratings of nine or ten.

Passives are satisfied but unenthusiastic customers who provide ratings of seven or eight.

Detractors are unhappy customers who give ratings from zero to six.[8]

Reichheld then suggested creating a "Net Promoter Score or NPS," which is calculated by taking the percentage of customers who are promoters and subtracting the percentage who are detractors. Some of the most successful companies—such as Amazon.com, eBay, Dell, Costco, USAA, Intuit, FedEx, Harley-Davidson, Vanguard, and Enterprise Rent-a-Car—have NPS ratings that range from 50 to 80 percent. However, the average firm sputters along with scores of only 5 to 10 percent. Some organizations have NPS ratings that are *negative!*[9]

Using data from Counting Opinions,[10] a firm that specializes in library data management solutions for libraries (including a customer satisfaction feedback management system), a NPS was calculated for a number of U.S. and Canadian public libraries. The NPS ratings ranged from a high of 73.2 percent to a low of 21.3 percent for public libraries, which, although good, offers real room for improvement.[11] And although calculating a NPS for your library might be revealing, it's not about the score but rather how you use the score to make improvements.

Thus, if a library is "satisfied" with just "satisfied" customers, then these customers may or may not come back to the library. Sure, their needs were met. The service was OK. The overall experience was OK—but nothing to write home about! Their overall feelings about the library are between neutral and positive—not bad, but not great!

The importance of providing ongoing training for library staff members cannot be overstated, because poorly trained employees will make mistakes. In such situations, customers will experience problems that are repeated over and over. One of the challenges for the library is that customers find it difficult to communicate with the library. Thus, rather than complain about poor service, they will more than likely simply walk away and never return.

The goal is to provide such high levels of service that customers will be delighted and become *raving enthusiasts* for the library. A loyal customer is one that has his or her needs met and exceeded. Your delivery was GREAT. The service was GREAT. The experience was GREAT. The customer's overall feelings about the library are enthusiastic and his or her experiences are memorable. So GREAT was the experience that the customer feels compelled to share it with others. WOW!

Interestingly, from 40 to as much as 60 percent of the customer satisfaction survey respondents will provide open-ended comments, both good and bad, about the library. The combination of the survey results plus the open-ended comments provides rich and immediate feedback on how well the library is doing—from the **customer's perspective.**

CONCLUSION

The importance of recruiting, training, and involving your staff members in co-creating a customer-focused library cannot be overstated. In the end, it is staff who will be delivering a set of services, and the manner in which they do this and their attitudes will determine—in the eyes of the customer—whether the library is successful.

One important question that each staff member should be asking is, "Are the things I am doing today really adding value to the lives of the customers of this library?"

Really good customer service comes from actions that make the customer's experience with your library one that exceeds their expectations. It is the

Attitude   *Caring*

Knowledge   Helpfulness

Responsiveness   Consistency

Concern   Courtesy

Enthusiasm   EXPERTISE

that staff members bring to their jobs in the delivery of the service for which they are responsible.

Quality customer service requires the

enthusiastic participation of every staff member.

NOTES

1. *Good to Great: Why Some Companies Make the Leap . . . and Others Don't* (New York: HarperCollins, 2001).

2. *Evaluating Training Programs: The Four Levels* (San Francisco: Berrett-Koehler, 2006).

3. Cathy De Rosa and Jenny Johnson, *From Awareness to Funding: A Study of Library Support in America* (Dublin, OH: OCLC, 2008), 1–6.

4. See the video for an entertaining and depressing review of how we embrace change in an organization, at www.youtube.com/watch?v=mKSvgmpVJFk.

5. *Managing Transitions: Making the Most of Change* (Reading, MA: Addison-Wesley, 1991).

6. *Dune* (Clifton Park, NY: Chilton Books, 1965), 76.

7. James Allen, Frederick F. Reichheld, Barry Hamilton, and Rob Markey, "Closing the Delivery Gap: How to Achieve True Customer-Led Growth," *Results Brief Newsletter, Bain & Company* (October 5, 2005).

8. "The One Number You Need to Grow," *Harvard Business Review* 82, no. 6 (June 2004): 46–54.

9. Fred Reichheld, *The Ultimate Question: Driving Good Profits and True Growth* (Boston: Harvard Business School Press, 2006).

10. For more information, visit www.CountingOpinions.Com.

11. Joseph R. Matthews, "Customer Satisfaction: A New Perspective," *Public Libraries* (November/December 2008): 52–55.

9

Removing the Shackles of Tradition

Settle for More!

—A pin worn by Karen McPheeters,
Library Director of the Farmington
Public Library, New Mexico

We must become the change we want to see.

—Mahatma Gandhi

Change is a door that can only be opened from the inside.

—Old French proverb

Reinventing a library is all about creating something that is daring, remarkable, and fun! The goal is to become a **WOW! Library,** and the idea is to delight the customer—again and again! To achieve this objective will require some "out-of-the-box" thinking. Fundamental to the reinvention process is to develop a clear understanding of the value proposition for each market segment the library is serving.

Unfortunately for most communities, "a library is a library is a library is a . . ." . The size and architectural style may be different, but inside, most libraries will have the same look and feel and provide the same set of services in essentially the same way. The time for some creativity and risk taking is NOW! It is time to reinvent your library! It is time to redefine what your library is!

The challenge is to create something that will be extraordinary and memorable. The library has to be unique, easily distinguished from its competitors, and create a range of services and a physical space that will make it a true destination—one whose

*There is a season for sitting on a porch and there is a season for action. The time for action is **now!***

appeal is so compelling that people are drawn to the library frequently. The goal is to make your customers exclaim WOW! when they visit your library—physically or virtually.

73

Too many libraries settle for a library that is "OK." Given that a library building will last from 30 years or more before it may be remodeled or replaced, clearly a library must build for tomorrow. Too many libraries have a vision that can be achieved too easily. Too often libraries will be constrained by a budget for building a library without getting creative or exploring other options for funding. Barbara Markuson, former director of INCOLSA, a library cooperative in Indiana, was fond of saying:

> "Librarians always have difficulty getting the money
> to do the job right the first time,
> but librarians never have difficulty getting the money
> to do a job over a second or third time!"

What then should a library do to reinvent itself? Jack of all trades, master of one, is what *Built to Last* author Jim Collins would label as the "power of the and."[1] Being a jack of all trades implies you can't also be the master of one. However, being remarkable *and* providing real value in the lives of a library's customers means doing *both*. Build bridges between your tower (that you master) and others.

Customers don't view a library as a collection of materials and service desks—be it circulation, reference, information, meeting rooms, magazines, the books, and so forth. They couldn't care less about how the library is structured and organized. What they want is an intuitive experience that draws them and excites and delights them. They want to be able to find what they are looking for without encountering obstacles and barriers.

What is really interesting about S. R. Ranganathan's Five Laws of Library Science[2] is their customer focus:

- **Books are for use.** Although seemingly obvious, books (and other materials) have not always been accessible to patrons at their libraries. And although books are no longer chained to shelves to prevent borrowing, it has not been uncommon for some libraries to have some portions of their collections closed to the public.

- **Every reader his or her book.** Any person clearly has a right to use the collections housed in the library. Collections should be developed that are responsive to the needs of each market segment.

- **Every book its reader**. Each book (or other type of material) in the library will be of interest—it is hoped—to someone in the community. Inherent in this law is the realization that the library should provide multiple ways to discover the book (beyond the library's OPAC).

- **Save the time of the reader**. This law has been forgotten in many libraries. It is time for libraries to remove the barriers to accessing the collection, whether browsing or searching for a specific item. Every activity in the library should be judged on whether we are saving the time and making things easier for the customer.

- **The library is a growing organism**. Change should be embraced in recognition of the fact that the community being served by the library is in a constant state of change. In addition, librarians should be excited at the prospect of participating in the process of reinventing the library.

WALK THE WALK!

I offer you a *walk the walk challenge*. Whether you are a library director, library manager, librarian, or library board member, take a walk in the shoes of your customers! However, before you begin, remember that your existing point of view is shaped by the knowledge and experience you have (and you have a lot when it comes to libraries). Herb Simon once observed, "One does not live for months or years in a particular position in an organization, exposed to some streams of communication, shielded from others, without the most profound effects upon what he knows, believes, attends to, hopes, wishes, emphasizes, fears, and proposes."[3] And Peter Drucker has noted, "The executive is within an organization. Every executive . . . sees the inside—the organization—as close and immediate reality. He sees the outside only through thick and distorting lenses, if at all. What goes on outside is usually not even known firsthand. It is received through an organizational filter of reports, that is, in an already predigested and highly abstract form."[4]

It can be very instructive to walk a mile in another's shoes—as long as we take off our own shoes and remove our thick and distorting lenses first! We are so influenced by our experiences that we find it difficult to see what is new or different. The past affects us so powerfully that we may be blind to new possibilities. We tend to see what we are used to seeing—or expect to see!

> *In the beginner's mind there are many possibilities; in the expert's mind there are few.*
> —Shunryu Suzuki[5]

The challenge for us is to go back and become a beginner so that we can see the library from the perspective of the customer—from the **outside in!** As you become a beginner, answer the following questions for your library:

- How easy is it to find the library and park your car?

- Is there a sign indicating the hours the library is open, clearly visible from the street?

- What is the physical appearance of the library?

- Enter through the library's front doors. Are you greeted?

- Is it easy to identify where the DVDs, CDs, or fiction or nonfiction books are located?

- What problems do you encounter if you rely solely on signage to find a space in the library? (Remember that you don't know where anything is.)

- Browse the collection looking for a DVD, a CD, or a book. Are the shelves really full? How long has it been since the collection was vigorously weeded?

- Is the library cluttered? Are there too many staff-generated signs?

- Use the library's online catalog. How simple or cluttered is the search screen compared to Google?

- Ask a staff member to place a hold on the number one best seller for you. How long (weeks or months) will you have to wait to receive a copy?

- Use a public computer to do your work for an hour or two. What is the condition of the computer? Are you comfortable in your surroundings?

- Can you find the restrooms without asking? Use the public restrooms several times a day. Are they clean? Do they smell pleasant?

- What is the process to reserve a meeting room?

- Does someone at the circulation desk say, "Thanks for visiting *your library*" when you check out or leave?

- Is there an attractive sign (flat panel screen) that informs people as they leave of upcoming library events and programs?

- Try calling the library before it opens. How friendly is the voice recording? Now call when the library is open. How many times must you make a choice before you actually speak to someone?

So, as you spent the day in the shoes of your customers, how many times did you get frustrated? When did touchpoints become "points of pain?"

WHERE TO START

Start with the customer's perspective, of course! Remember that it is the customer—first, last, and always! Yet too often a library's planning process is inward looking rather than really focusing on the library's customers. The answer isn't technology, because technology is just a means to an end. Rather, the focus should be on the service model. What services will be offered, and how will they be delivered?

The majority of library staff members are so busy every day on the phone, using a computer, in meetings, and so forth that their *behinds* are facing the customers. After awhile staff begin to focus on what is happening in their department rather than on what concerns the customer. If all library staff members considered their own departmental activities as always secondary to the needs of the customer, then it would be natural for staff to think of the customer first.

It is imperative that library staff get out of the library and get involved in the lives of the community so that they will better understand that the library is not the center of people's lives. Most important, it is crucial that libraries recognize that they are serving various market segments of the population and not all members of the community. Thus, it is critical to develop a deep understanding of the needs of each market segment.

Everything you do should be to make the library less annoying.

In recent years Procter & Gamble (P&G) have reinvented themselves and now employees, managers, and even the president of the company spend time with customers of P&G products—for days at a time. Many of these visits are videoed so that they can be shared with other managers and employees. The result has been very positive in terms of customer satisfaction and P&G financial results.

This immersive activity, sometimes called *ethnography*, results in deep customer insights and leads to developing products and services that will truly delight library customers. This immersion in the lives of customers and closely observing their behaviors allows any organization, including public libraries, to address the needs of various customer segments in ways customers would never be able to articulate on their own. Immersing yourself in the customer's wider world of culture and daily activities gives you the opportunity of developing services that will truly delight and WOW the customer.

As library staff members immerse themselves in the lives of their customers, they will immediately realize that no "one" customer is representative of all customers. Rather, there are a number of customer types or market segments, each of which must be clearly understood. The bottom line is that you must first really understand a problem rather than immediately begin to seek a solution.

Understanding the problem is, in large part, all about understanding the library's value proposition for each market segment. Imagine library staff, at all levels, are so focused on the customer that they help pull the **outside-in** by

sending out staff to become engaged in the lives of customers;

bringing in customers to learn from them;

using relevant data to put the spotlight on customers, how they use the library, and the value they derive from such use;

listening to customer-facing employees;

sharing widely what is learned about each customer segment;

creating a persona (and perhaps a video) about each market segment; and

talking constantly about the need for urgency in learning more about the customers!

So what does a customer-focused library look like? Well, if we invert the traditional organizational pyramid, as shown in Figure 9.1, we wind up with something much more appropriate. At the top are the library's customers! First, foremost, and always, it's about the customer. Customers sometimes interact with customer-interfacing staff, and it is through these interchanges or "moments of truth" that the library staff determine what kind of experience the customer has. Will the customer leave the library saying "WOW! What a great library!", or will the reaction be indifference or anger? ("I am NOT coming back to this library!")

Supporting the customer-facing staff are the remaining staff, or support staff. The customers of the support staff are the customer-facing staff. Their job is to ensure that the customer-facing staff have the tools, training, and resources to deliver a WOW experience. The library management team is next; their job is to ensure that everyone remembers that they are there to serve the interests and needs of the customer. Below the library management team is the library director, who is ultimately responsible for making sure that everyone "gets" the fact that the customer is the king! Reporting to a library board, in many cases, the library director ensures that the board and other interested stakeholders are informed about the success that the library is having in meeting the needs of the community.

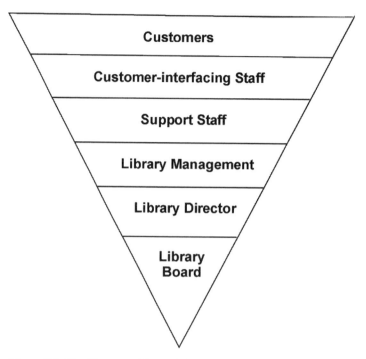

Figure 9.1. The Customer-Focused Library Organizational Diagram

MISSION/VISION

Historically libraries have defined themselves by, and continue to report statistics about, the number and range of items on shelves and the equipment (computer workstations) they provide. In addition to input measures, libraries have also reported the amount of use of the library (output measures). In reality, libraries should be having conversations with their funding decision makers about the services they deliver, the experiences and personal growth they enable, and the contributions of the library to individuals in the community.

If your public library wishes to embrace a broader role in the community, then it most likely will have to learn more about the needs of the individuals who live in the community. The Singapore Public Library spent two years meeting with a number of individuals, conducting many focus groups, and holding a number of community forums to discuss the future of the library. The end result was a mission/vision that had two broad aims:

• Assist in improving the educational levels of the islands population.

• Contribute to the economic development of the community.

When engaged in the planning process, there are two basic approaches. You can start from where the library is today and work forward (the approach most libraries choose), or you can start with a picture of the future and figure out what it will take to get you there.

When you start from where you are today, you make the assumption that the library staff, tools, and systems currently in place will grow at the proper rate and in the direction of your ultimate goal. That is a big assumption, especially if you want to make some significant changes. Remember that the library's current mode of operations has been to help maintain and solidify the status quo.

If you start with a picture of the future and wor backward, you can figure out what it will take to get you there. This allows the library to identify what must be changed to create this vision.

EMBRACE INNOVATION

Becoming a customer-focused library is not going to be an easy and straightforward activity. It is going to take concerted action by a great many individuals to embrace the vision and sign on to a significant amount of change.

Nearly all accounts of deep change, regardless of the organizational setting, suggest that the change is crisis-led, episodic, and programmatic. Implementing change is typically accomplished through a top-to-bottom torrent of scripted messages, events, goals, and actions. Rarely is change opportunity-led, continuous, and a product of the organization's intrinsic capacity to learn and adapt. The need for organizations to innovate and adopt transformational change into the organizations' DNA has long been advocated. Peter Drucker noted in 1995, "Every organization of today has to build into its very structure the *management of change* . . . . It has to build in *organized abandonment* of everything it does.[6] The challenge to transformational change, of course, is to overcome incrementalism (making small changes to existing facilities and service offerings), which continues to prevail among library directors, administrators, board members, and elected officials. Your library must develop a capacity for candid self-reflection to see its strengths and weaknesses—as your customers see them.

Despite these challenges, this is exactly what public libraries must do. It is time for your public library to implement a series of innovative strategies and services that will have broader appeal to the communities you serve. The change must be radical rather than evolutionary (more of the same simply will not do). Innovation must focus on increasing the capacity of library customers to do what they want and need to do in the way that most benefits their productivity (by saving the customers' time), pleasure, and pursuit of knowledge.

Challenging the traditional view of library services in an attempt to better understand customers so that you can reinvent your library will require that you ask a series of questions—repeatedly. Among these are the following:

- Is this a library-centric tradition, and should it be challenged? Does it get in the way of considering other options for delivering library services?

- Does this belief apply to all public libraries? Are there counter examples? What is the experience of other libraries that have attempted alternatives?

- Does this belief serve the interests of the customer, or of library staff members? What are the implications for library customers if an alternative is implemented?

- Do the choices and assumptions that we make about what a library is become a self-fulfilling prophecy? Can we imagine alternatives?

- Are the alternatives we are considering bold enough? Do they represent a significant departure from traditional library practices? Have the library's competitors embarked on new service delivery models?

Figure 9.2 (p. 80) provides a simplified overview of the innovation cycle. Notice that central to the whole concept is *listening* to your customers. If a library is going to innovate and experiment to deliver a WOW experience to the public library customer, then it needs to be creative at several different levels.

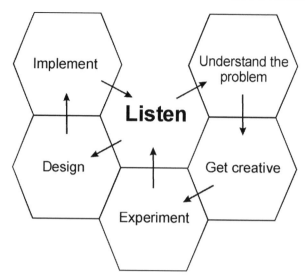

Figure 9.2. Innovation Cycle

A library can consider strategy alternatives when it really *listens* to its customers so that it can *understand the problem* and then *get creative* and *conduct experiments* in an effort to really deliver value to the customer:

- *Strategy.* A strategy is a choice, among several options, for how a library is going to accomplish a specific goal. As noted previously, the exploration of strategic options rarely occurs when a library does "strategic planning." Rather, a library will establish a series of goals and objectives within the context of the "same old thing." The "look and feel" of the library seldom changes. The choice of a strategy will determine the extent to which innovation is embraced and explored.

- *Management.* One of the greatest challenges for library management is to recognize that they do not know all the answers. They need to encourage a great many people to make suggestions about the future directions for the library. This means that they will have to carefully *listen*—for example, try not to say anything in a meeting for 20 to 30 minutes. Managers have to listen to staff members. (The folks at the lower levels in the organization will often have unconventional views, which makes it difficult to get a hearing or even have their ideas considered on their merits.) Similarly, library management will have to be involved in the lives of their customers to better understand their needs.

  Do not assume that what has worked well in the past is the best approach for the present. Inattention to competing and often conflicting viewpoints may lead to some poor decisions. Yet the maxim "learn fast, fail fast" clearly holds true. Libraries must *experiment* with various service delivery models and share their experiences—good and bad—with their colleagues. Consider alternative ways to *design* the delivery of a service and then work hard to *implement* the design. The reality, however, is that libraries are much too complacent and that librarians are reluctant to admit it. As noted by John Kotter, we need to develop and maintain a sense of urgency![7]

  It is also important to acknowledge that there will be many twists and turns on the innovation and experimentation highway. It is not a straight-line process, but rather is irregular and angular and seemingly proceeds, at times, without a sense of direction.

Recognize that innovation is a series of approximations to the future. Learn by experimenting, then evaluate and make mid-course adjustments as needed.

- *Service.* How library staff members interact with library customers will determine whether the customer is delighted or frustrated. The choice of language during a conversation to explain library policies is very important. Whether the staff member is sitting behind a service desk or is roaming the library will contribute to a very different experience—from the customer's perspective. Body language is also very important—eye contact, a smile, a nod—in establishing positive interaction with customers.

- *Operations.* A library must ensure that it is operating as efficiently as possible. It should examine whether all of the tasks and activities it routinely performs are still adding value. And similarly, it should be exploring different ways of accomplishing the same tasks, which may mean outsourcing.

Because the leadership of the library director and the top management team is so important to creating an environment that is supportive of innovation, it might be instructive to determine whether your library's leadership is

- energetic and creative rather than preserving the status quo;

- participatory and caring rather than elitist;

- motivated by mission and vision rather than by tradition;

- listening, coaching, and mentoring rather than supervising; and

- personally demonstrating the library's values or institutionalizing policies.

A director or formal management group may be the most visible leader, but most libraries have leaders throughout the organization. Innovative organizations seem to have a larger number of change agents and idea champions. The challenge is to create a culture that empowers them to act. These individual innovation champions are extremely important leaders in building staff buy-in and nurturing ideas.

Not surprisingly, there are many ways to crush innovation and perpetuate a culture of inertia. Among the more popular and easy to recognize methods to crush innovation are

- saying, "We tried that once!" or "We don't . . ., haven't . . ., won't . . ., can't . . .";

- requesting a formal written proposal;

- creating a committee;

- saying "It will never fly" or "The climate isn't right" or "Don't ruffle any feathers" or "If it ain't broke, don't fix it!" or "That isn't even your department" or "You will get laughed out of the room" or "That's too risky" or "Don't step on any toes";

- scheduling a meeting;

- saying, "That's a silly idea! Why would you suggest that?"; and

- saying, "Yes, but . . .".[8]

THE IMPORTANCE OF DESIGN

The process of design consists of looking at the same thing everyone else is but thinking something different. Design is most frequently associated with a product or the packages that contain the product, but design can also play an important part in how people interact with their surroundings in a building as well as at various points of service contact. Whether you are constructing a new building or remodeling an existing one, it is important to acknowledge that design goes beyond the services that an architect can provide.

Design is about the total customer experience, not simply the layout and arrangement of shelving, furnishing, and rooms. Too often a library is involved with "silent design"—the design of services without the benefit of a discipline of service design. Good design is about capturing and communicating ideas in a way that draws people in and makes connections.

As shown in Figure 9.3, design can be used to improve the physical facilities, the preparation of customer-facing staff, and the service delivery process.

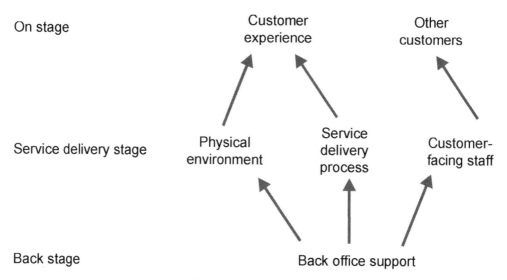

Figure 9.3. Design Areas

Design involves developing a clear understanding of the needs of the customer (often through field observations), brainstorming to develop a set of possibilities, selecting one or two ideas, and rapidly developing prototypes to obtain the reactions of real customers. This feedback helps shape further revisions to the prototypes and even more feedback. Recently, Apple turned to designers to create a whole new look and feel for its showrooms and stores, with very positive results.

In the absence of detailed information about our customers, we all work from assumptions about who the customer is, what the customer does in the library, and what the customer knows about the library. Following these assumptions, we tend to design for ourselves and not for the customer.

When a problem crops up, consider it a design opportunity. Look at the problem from several perspectives, but most important, from the customer's perspective—from the

outside-in!

All services are experienced over time. People take different journeys to, through, and from a service. Good service design recognizes these differences and examines what happens before, during, and after the service experience, for both library staff members and the customer. Exploring the different emotional journeys that people take through a service is also a powerful way to segment service users to directly inform redesign.

MAYA Design, a consulting firm, helped the Carnegie Library of Pittsburgh better understand that from the customer's perspective, a library is a very complex organization. The MAYA team used a variety of tools, such as focus groups, shadowing, direct observation, and developing personas, to better understand the user's mental model and the library's organizational schemes. Using information architecture, the team identified three ways of organizing information: space, people, and categorizations (e.g., Dewey). All this effort resulted in identifying a number of points at which a customer "touchpoint" failed, as shown in Figure 9.4 (p. 84). These breaking points were the result of a customer failing to understand library jargon, encountering an organizational complexity (typified by failing to find or understand signage), having difficulty in using a library-provided tool, and so forth. The result is that the remodeled library facilities and library Web site in Pittsburgh have now become a destination, as evidenced by an increase in the gate count, circulation, and attendance at programs.

Service is a key part of the customer experience. The service experienced by a customer is not a one-time event, but rather a journey that consists of numerous touchpoints between the customer and the organization. These touchpoints must be carefully designed and managed; each touchpoint has a potential for innovation. Some organizations are turning to "service designers" to help shape the best possible customer experience. A great library experience must incorporate the totality of the organization. Do everything right but get one touchpoint wrong, and you've eliminated the possibility for delivering a great experience. Clearly the design of the library experience will ultimately determine what happens at the service touchpoints and how the service is delivered.

Great design delights and results in smiles and compliments. It results in customers coming back again and again. Great design generates wonderful word-of-mouth recommendations and endorsements. It results in a win for everyone—the library and the customer.

Design thinking isn't limited to products. Systems also require great design. And *everything* is a system. Your entire library is a system. Your customer service is a system. Your children's department is a system. Your checkout area—whether physical or electronic—is a system. Great systems are based on great design, and great design is based on observation: Putting yourself in your customers' shoes; understanding what they experience, not what you think happens; and finding ways of delighting them, or at the very least fulfilling their specific needs, should be driving the vision for your library.

Peter Morville has suggested that a good customer experience can be conceptualized in the "User Experience Honeycomb," shown in Figure 9.5 (p. 85).

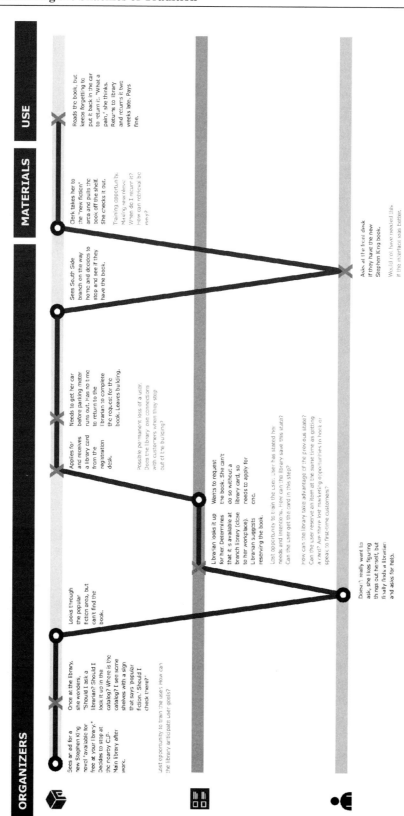

Figure 9.4. Customer Touchpoints in a Library Setting. Courtesy of MAYA Design.

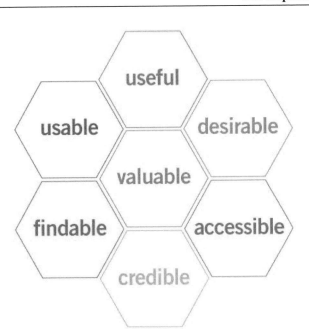

Figure 9.5. User Experience Honeycomb. Adapted from Peter Morville, *User Experience Honeycomb*, available at www.semanticstudios.com/publications/semantics/000029.php.

The facets of the user experience are the following:

- **Useful**. It is important to view the library's products and services from the customer's perspective. It may be necessary to really explore the value or utility of a library service to ensure that it really resonates with the customer.

- **Usable**. Ease of use remains central to the customer experience, so the library should focus on wayfinding—be it in the physical building or on the library's virtual Web site. Although usability is important, it is not the only facet of a great customer experience.

- **Desirable**. The sense of comfort and well-being is influenced greatly by the colors, sounds, and odors in the library building. In addition, the library brand—and every library has one—will influence people's perceptions of the library as a desirable destination.

- **Findable**. The library must ensure that it is easy to navigate both in the building and on the library's Web site. Where things are located must be very clear so that customers can find what they need.

- **Accessible**. Libraries have been fairly concerned about making sure that buildings have the necessary design features and equipment so that people with disabilities (about 10 percent of the population) are encouraged to use the library. The same should be true of a library's Web site.

- **Credible**. One of the strengths of a library is that people could count on finding quality resources and, over time, the library built up a reputation for being trustworthy.

- **Valuable**. The library must deliver value, real benefits, in the lives of our customers. What that value proposition is differs depending on why people come to the library.

Use these seven facets for evaluating customers' experiences when they visit the library or the library's Web site. Ask your customers, lots of customers, to do the same thing. The results will surprise you (and most likely discourage you). But the great thing is that you can change things to make the experience of visiting the library truly delightful and memorable.

The typical approach to problem solving is to first clearly understand the problem, then explore alternatives and assess the strengths and weaknesses of each alternative, and then make a decision and proceed with implementation. Design thinking approaches the problem from a different perspective. A broad group of customers is invited to explore an opportunity (the problem) and to brainstorm to develop a list of fresh ideas. The selection of several ideas is then shared with a group of customers, who then co-create the opportunity, and in an iterative manner prototypes are developed, until the opportunity really resonates with customers.

Designing a library experience from the perspective of the customer has been called *empathic design*. Rather than focusing on how a customer will interact with the library at one touchpoint, be aware that people's emotional, physical, and analytical needs should be met.

The analytical needs are intellectual and might involve selecting the right book or DVD, participating in an engaging program, getting assistance to answer a question, or interacting with others. The physical needs are a bit more challenging. After all, the library is not a gym, and you don't visit a library to work up a sweat! (Although mothers checking out a large number of picture books for their child might disagree.) However, physical needs also have to do with the physical characteristics of the library and how welcoming and inviting the experience is.

Emotional needs can be met in a variety of ways. For some, visiting the library can engender almost a spiritual reverence; for others, the ability to meet kindred souls makes the library the place to be. In short, is your library a destination that appeals to people on all three levels?

THE KEY

The key to designing a library and all of its library experiences is for the library to really understand the value proposition of the library. How does the library add value to the lives of its customers? Clearly the library is not the center of the customer's universe, but rather one of many places an individual can physically or virtually visit. The center of the universe, from the customer's perspective, is the customer! The reality is that the library has many competitors, and it has to acknowledge and understand their value proposition. Thus, the library has to find the "sweet spot" in the lives of its customers, as shown in Figure 9.6.

The library's "sweet spot" is somewhat similar to the three circles of the hedgehog concept described by Jim Collins in *Good to Great*:[9]

What can you be the best at in the world?

What you are deeply passionate about?

What provides value to your customers so that they in turn drive your organization's success?

When the public library truly becomes the customer's library, the customers will be telling wonderful stories about the library to their friends, work colleagues, relatives, the city manager, members of the city council, and so forth.

Remember that good is simply not "good enough!" Always deliver an experience that is more than was promised—in short, under-promise and over-deliver. The goal is to WOW the customer!

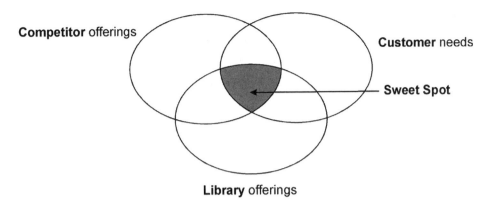

Figure 9.6. The Library Sweet Spot

Increasingly one of the most important reasons for using the services of any organization is convenience. The question then becomes for any library: Are we maintaining the library's traditional barriers to access, or are we actively working to make things easier to use and more convenient from the customer's perspective? Is the library becoming more valuable in the lives of our customers so that they have a compelling reason to visit, physically or virtually, again and again?

CONCLUSION

Deciding to create a customer-focused library in your community will be the start of a very exciting journey. Implicit in this journey is the reality that the library will be embracing a great deal of change. It is incumbent for the library director and the top management team to consider

how to change,

when to change,

at what velocity to change,

how to effectively manage and navigate change,

identifying the end result of change (the goals), and

determining the library's capability and requirements for change.

A customer-focused library can be created in a small, medium, or large library. Regardless of the size of your library, there are some important truths that should be acknowledged right up front. A customer-focused library will

- listen to its customers in a variety of ways;
- involve customers and staff in planning its services;
- be flexible and recognize that it is embracing change in many ways;
- recognize that some things that libraries have always done will have to be abandoned;
- acknowledge that digital content will assume much more importance over time;
- understand that no job will be unchanged;

- embrace participatory, user-driven services;
- keep things simple, streamlining and simplifying systems and procedures;
- deliver access to physical collections that is responsive to customer needs;
- understand that risk and experimentation are necessary;
- provide services and spaces that are welcoming;
- ensure that wayfinding is simple to understand;
- realize that technology is a means for delivering great service;
- provide a library Web site that is "in synch" with visiting the library;
- never be satisfied, always looking for things to do even better and blazing new trails;
- make pictures of people the artwork in the library and be storyteller;
- give time to the community, encouraging staff members to serve the community together;
- celebrate to create memories, smiling more and laughing (It's fun!); and
- realize that it must have an explicit, customer-based reason for everything it does!

Remember,

You don't have the answers—and

probably don't even know the questions!

But we both know someone that does.

That's right—**the customer!**

In the end,

the **only** perspective

that matters is

the customer's!

NOTES

1. James Collins and Jerry Porras, *Built to Last: Successful Habits of Visionary Companies* (New York: Harper Business, 1994).

2. Shiyali Ranganathan, *The Five Laws of Library Science* (London: Edward Goldston, 1931).

3. Herbert A. Simon, *Administrative Behavior* (New York: Free Press, 1945).

4. Quoted in Jeffrey Krames, *Inside Drucker's Brain* (New York: Portfolio, 2008).

5. Shunryû Suzuki, *Zen Mind, Beginner's Mind* (San Francisco: Shambhala Publications, 2006), 1.

6. *Post-Capitalist Society* (New York: HarperCollins, 1995), 57.

7. *A Sense of Urgency* (Boston: Harvard Business School Publishing, 2008).

8. Adapted from David Donathan, "10 Simple Rules for Crushing Innovation and Maintaining a Culture of Inertia," *University Business* (July 2008). Available at www.universitybusiness.com/viewarticle.aspx?articleid=1086&p=1#0.

9. *Good to Great: Why Some Companies Make the Leap . . . and Others Don't* (New York: HarperCollins, 2001), 89.

Index

About the Author

Joseph R. Matthews is a consultant specializing in strategic planning, assessment, and evaluation of library services; the use of performance measures; and the Library Balanced Scorecard. He was an instructor at the San Jose State University School of Library and Information Science and lives in Carlsbad, California.